ELEGANT SIMPLICITY

What you do not know is the only thing you know,
And what you own is what you do not own,
And where you are is where you are not,
Leading to a condition of complete simplicity,
Costing not less than everything.

T. S. Eliot

ELEGANT SIMPLICITY

Reflections on an Alternative Way of Being

JOHN REED

Designed by Louise Millar

Published by Calder Walker Associates
2 Umbria Street
London SW15 5DP
alangw@copperstream.co.uk

Printed by Bell & Bain,
Glasgow G46 7UQ

ISBN 978 0 9541275 5 8

Front cover illustration
by Marie Courtay

I dedicate this book to the memory of
my maternal grandfather, Dr Floriano de Lemos,
who devoted his life to treating the poor and needy
of Rio de Janeiro, Brazil. This modest and selfless
humanitarian was the very embodiment
of 'elegant simplicity'

Very special thanks are due for the assistance of
my wife, Dominique and my sons Peter and James.
I also value the wise council of
Serge Beddington-Behrens, Alan Gordon Walker
and Alasdair Forbes and I thank them
for their contribution

Author's Note

Most of what I have written in these reflections emerges from the experience of my personal egoism dancing and jousting through the course of an eventful life with urges of a more spiritual nature. This adventure, (complemented by readings of the Perennial Philosophy), have been my only true education. It is from personal experience, therefore, that I can say that egoism doesn't deliver on its promise. There is a deceptive quality to the allure of a narrowly egoistic vision of life that I would challenge anyone to prove to the contrary. Victories are fleeting and hollow when the heart is not open and when life is viewed from the prism of one's needs and desires alone.

In spite of the commonplace appearance to the contrary, the serene and humanly fulfilled egoist is an illusion. I am not naïve enough to believe that we shall collectively relinquish our egos and create a 'new Jerusalem' on earth. Sticking to the logic of self-interest we are all familiar with, I argue in favour of a more effective and positive form of selfishness, one in which our real needs are better served than by the ego and where our ultimate fulfillment can lie.

Foreword
Dr Serge Beddington-Behrens, PhD

I was delighted to be asked to write the foreword to this important book, as I have been a close friend of the author for over fifty years, and I have therefore been privy to observing the ideas explored here, quietly marinating inside him. What gives these words power and authenticity is that they emerge out of the integrity of John's heart, his own life always having been the alter upon which he has conducted his own experimentation into truth. Thus, over the years, he has gradually evolved his own brand of Elegant Simplicity, having won most of his battles (which we are all called to wage) against the many seductive pulls in our society that instruct us to 'sell our souls to the company store'!

Basically John's thesis is that we need to re-claim our hearts and souls; we are challenged to live more simply and elegantly, and that this is the only way forward, if, as a species, we are to survive. However, we cannot effectively do this unless we first come to understand how ugly and convoluted our current world has become. Or as a character in a Thomas Mann novel once put it: 'If a way to the better there be, it lies in our taking a full look at the worst.' And this is precisely what John helps us to do. He does not pull any punches. He points out, as spiritual teachers have been doing since time immemorial, that our major stumbling block is that we believe that who we are, is what our egos tell us who we are! And the problem is that this view of the world is always a reductive and jaundiced one (our egos being 'clever' but not intelligent, 'always dwelling on the past and the future but never able to be in present time'.)

Therefore, so long as we live through our egotisms, we remain cut off from who we really are and thus suffer from what John calls 'societal de-spiritualisation'. Where there is no inner life, 'one passes into the power of outer life completely. Man becomes a helpless creature of mass movements, mass-politics, of gigantic mass-organisations.' What we need to learn to do, he tells us, is to move beyond our ego identities, so that we are no longer run by agendas impelling us to devote our lives only to becoming rich, glorious, famous and powerful. Instead, we are called to discover the authentic us. Only if we change inwardly and begin to do this, the author reminds us, can changes occur in our outer world.

The book is full of profound and rich observations into the anomalies of our modern culture. Here are just a couple of them: 'In the 20th century we were liberated from the yoke of material want only to find ourselves now enslaved by the needs and desires that come with material abundance'. Commenting on what is amiss in the work place, he observes that 'we throw our resources into financial activities that generate high private rewards disproportionate to their social productivity'! Such truisms pepper every page.

Whether John is decrying the lack of true statesmanship in our world leaders, the way 'modern' art has degenerated, or how prone we are to eat badly, everything he says is of crucial importance and this book is a 'must' not only for those who want actively to 'make a difference' but also for people who simply need to be clearer about civilisation and its many discontents. And it will certainly help them as this is very clearly written. I suggest you read it slowly and ponder over each sentence carefully, and that you continually ask yourself: 'Do any of the author's observations apply to me?'

For well they might! And if so, celebrate the fact. We cannot make changes in our lives unless we are very clear on what needs changing. This is a book about society, but since society is always a reflection of ourselves, it is also a book about you and me!

Introduction

I have been justifiably criticised for being excessively negative about the state of the world and for giving insufficient mention of the good and true in our midst. I acknowledge this wholeheartedly. Undoubtedly there are many wonderful, wise and dedicated people doing heroic and selfless work in the world. A tribute to these 'Warriors of the Heart', as my friend Dr. Serge Beddington-Behrens describes them, is long overdue and deserves a book in itself, which he is writing now and which will soon be finished. I have not developed this positive side of the picture for one main reason. To have done so to the extent it deserves, would, I felt, dilute the impact of the clarion call for change that was my intention.

Much personal transformation has taken place in the world. At a grass roots level, in spite of the appearance to the contrary, a movement for change is gathering form. Eckhart Tolle writes about this in a hopeful and inspiring manner in his book *A New Earth*. Millions have begun to be disenchanted with an egoistic way of life and have quietly and without fanfare established saner and less selfish habits of being. Clearly, this reflection is not directed at them. They are aware of all this already. It is only by enlarging their ranks, however, that we can arrive at a point where change will evolve organically in the world as a reflection of the soul-based urge of each one of us. This, unfortunately, is not the case yet. As things are, we are on a collision course with a socio-economic and ecological disaster of an unprecedented nature. *The Titanic* has hit the iceberg but the majority of passengers has not understood the gravity of the situation and is still dancing in the ballrooms. My hope is that by demonstrating the relevance of the wisdom teachings in the context of current events in the world, this reflection will have meaning to those who would not ordinarily be interested in esoteric or spiritual matters. It is *their* change of heart that the world needs so urgently.

I

An Indian Professor of Economics stood up at the Davos Forum some years ago and said that the emerging countries of the world should not aspire to western standards of living but that we should all learn to live in elegant simplicity'. At the time this struck me as an unusually wise statement and one that I felt would probably not be understood by the majority of luminaries at the forum. Events since have proved it to be extremely prescient. It is now becoming increasingly clear that the world cannot continue along the growth trajectory of the past and that the inherent contradictions of our socio-economic order and the impoverished spiritual condition of Man, of which it is a reflection, are now causing us serious problems. The near collapse of the financial system in September of 2008 is only a symptom of dysfunction at the heart of our way of living and being. By resurrecting the same patterns in the future as have failed in the past, these deep-rooted anomalies will not go away and can only get worse. At present, the intention of governments worldwide is a rapid return to 'business as usual' by massive programmes of financial stimulation to resuscitate demand. The likely failure of these policies will force people to understand that the socio-economic challenges we face today are of a different nature altogether. Only a profound modification in our conception of the meaning and purpose of life can see us through this enduring crisis successfully.

The rising crescendo of egoism of the last half-century presaged our troubles today. After the Second World War, French Minister of Culture, Andre Malraux, was famously reported to have declared that 'the 21st Century will be spiritual or it will not be'. Given the context at that time, he was probably referring to the danger of nuclear extinction. The threat of financial and ecological breakdown probably would have seemed remote. All of these possibilities exist today and always for the same reasons. The excessive way in which we, as individuals or collectively as nations, advance our selfish interests is and has always been at the root of all our personal and societal problems. Malraux no doubt recognised that these contradictions could not continue indefinitely, and that, we either master our egoistic ways by some form of moral transcendence or they would prove to be our undoing. *That time is now.* With six and a half billion people on earth, we know that we can't dispense with a system of economic organisation such as capitalism. We have experimented with alternative systems without success. Since it was our limitless expectations that gave rise to the excesses and abuses we are witnessing today, there is no reason to believe that, by modifying those expectations, we can't alter the nature of capitalism to our ultimate benefit. The new balance and moderation in habits of living and being implied by the idea of 'elegant simplicity' is an invitation to explore these possibilities.

II

The underlying rational for capitalism has always been that each person, by pursuing his or her self-interest, would contribute to the good of the whole. This idea has been accepted as a self-evident truth by the modern world. At the heart of this belief lies the conviction that the satisfaction of our material needs and desires lead to individual happiness. In fact, the right to the unhampered pursuit of such happiness is the cornerstone of the American Constitution and the foundation of the 'American way of life'. But is this really true? Do material comforts make us happy? The evidence would suggest that this has been a flawed concept from the start. In every spiritual tradition going back thousands of years, we have been told in different ways that 'man does not live by bread alone', which is to say, that we also have spiritual needs that cannot be answered by material means alone.

In every attempt to establish a workable vision of society, this central truth has never been given the consideration it deserves. Our liberal capitalist model is the culminating example. Centuries of materialism at the expense of the spirit are now causing it to unravel from the weight of its contradictions. Sub-prime problems and greedy bankers are merely the symptoms of this disorder. They are not the cause. Rapacity and greed have dominated history. There is nothing new about all this. In the middle ages the subjugating power of the Church made religious practice a crude and perverse caricature of spirituality. In subsequent centuries, material progress was achieved to the benefit of the few by oppressing the many. Finally, in the 20th Century we were liberated, in the West, at least, from the yoke of material want, only to find ourselves enslaved by the needs and desires that come with material abundance. What all these epochs have in common is the essential de-spiritualisation of society. The great mystical teachings never took root. We long ago gave up our souls hoping to 'gain the whole world'.

Quite recently, in a moment of extraordinary hubris, it was widely asserted that the free-market system, by being globalised, would ultimately cure the woes of the world. Such enthusiasm even gave rise to the view by Francis Fukyama, Professor of International Political Economics at John Hopkins University, that we had achieved the 'End of History', meaning that democratic capitalism could never be surpassed as a socio-political model of society! Now that it is clear that this assessment was somewhat premature, are we any closer to recognising that we must re-appropriate our souls so as to establish a more balanced and enduring concept of society? Not yet, I don't believe, but we will be under increasing pressure to do so in the years ahead. Belief and confidence in our established ways of living is beginning to falter but we don't know what 'model' of society to turn to. We don't know where to find meaning. 'Soul' is and will always be the expression of our spiritual nature. It's what enables us to 'sense' our way to the essential meaning of things. Without it we are unregulated by the spirit and become destructive to ourselves and to the planet we live in. What we see happening around us today is the result of this disconnection. C. G. Jung, one of the fathers of modern psychiatry, made these important observations:

> When you study the mental history of the world, you see that people in times immemorial had a general teaching or doctrine about the wholeness of the world. In our civilisation this spiritual background has gone astray. Our Christian doctrine has lost its grip to an appalling extent, largely because people don't understand it anymore. Thus one of the most important instinctual activities of mind has lost its object. As these views deal with the world as a whole, they create also a wholeness of the individual... **Among all my patients in the second half of life every one of them fell ill because he had lost what the living religions of the past have given their followers, and none of them has been really healed who did not regain his spiritual outlook.**[1]

III

But what is it that we need to understand so as to re-activate our souls? In essence the message has always been the same. The millennial spiritual teachings (the Perennial Philosophy) tell us that we are part of an intelligent energy force or collective consciousness that we can loosely call 'God'. Our presence on earth in body and mind tempt us to believe that we live as separate and distinct entities. The identification with this sense of separateness gives rise to the ego. This illusion at the core of our beings has continuously robbed us of our true inner identity and with it, our capacity to live to the fullest expression of what it is to be human. The failure to rise above our egoistic ways has fashioned a 'civilisation' far less glorious than we would like to believe, and one that will slowly destroy itself. That process is currently underway.

There is not a single human failing that cannot be attributed to the ego. Whether it's your boss taking credit for your hard work, a name dropped by someone to draw attention to themselves, Richard Branson's unique style of self-promotion or simply, your husband, wife, or friend who can't admit that he or she is wrong about something, the ego is invariably the culprit. What is the true nature of this psychological anomaly, how and why does it arise and what can be done to diminish its power over us? In answer to these fundamental questions, the wisdom teachings have been proposing remedies for thousands of years. Tibetan Buddhists, for example, encourage us to examine our motives for what we do or say at all times. In practice, which is not easy, this exercise can be very effective. Lurking behind much of what we do and say lies the desire to be perceived by others in a favourable light. As obvious and normal as this may sound, very few people recognise the degree to which the need to be liked, loved or respected rules their lives depriving them of psychological independence. To become conscious of this underlying dynamic, as the Buddhists suggest, is to change it. Furthermore, it helps us to understand, in a way that would not otherwise be possible, that the world we have created, often dysfunctional, violent and unjust, is the collective consequence of this way of being. From this arises a very common 'blind spot'. We lament the way things are without acknowledging that, in seemingly small and indefinable ways, we contribute to them. After all, if we are not collectively responsible for things being as they are, who is?

Take, for example, the case of people who lose their jobs. They are instantly plunged into a black hole of self-doubt and loss of self-esteem. Never mind that the personal qualities that he or she possesses are essentially the same before as after the event, somehow their sense of self-worth suddenly alters dramatically. The inner identity that defines our personal human worth independent of the vagaries of life is absent. We are then condemned to live life as a slavish hostage to our pride. Who in the normal conditions of life in our driven western societies can honestly say that this isn't the case? Can this diminished inner state be the fruit of thousands of years of 'civilisation'? Is it the best we can expect from men and women 'made in the image of God'? The answer, fortunately, is no. We are separated from our veritable nature by conditioned habits of egoism that is within our power to change. There is nothing new about this. The mystical teachings have been bearing this message for millennia. Modern western mystics such as Ram Das or Eckhart Tolle, by telling us 'to be here now' or to 'be present', are doing the same thing. To be 'present' is to be 'awake' to your authentic and intrinsic self — free of ego. For most people, however, the idea that we sail through life asleep to ourselves gives rise to an apparent paradox that remains a huge obstacle to their being able to accept this fact. How is it that a person can be highly effective in the world, run corporations or countries, send rockets to the moon and still be 'asleep'? Similarly, with all the intelligence that exists in the world, the kind that splits atoms and creates the Internet, we are rarely able to find enduring solutions to the major moral and psychological issues in our lives. The explanation is the same in both cases.

Intelligence based on reason alone, no matter how clever, has its limitations. Einstein himself said that he couldn't have arrived at an understanding of the Principle of Relativity without breaking through to an intuitive form of thought beyond the purely rational and empirical. Knowing and understanding must reveal not only the how but also the why, which is to say, the *meaning* of things. This is a spiritual not an intellectual experience alone, the brain being only a part of the equation. The spirit, heart, soul, whatever you choose to call it, is the other part. Only the combination of the two produces real understanding, the kind that carries absolute certainty within itself. This, however, is a mystical fact, not a scientific one, and, as with all mystical certitudes, it can be *experienced* but not explained in scientific terms. Why should this provoke so much scepticism? After all, isn't the experience of something more important than its explanation? The conventional answer is no. Rationalism has decreed that no such experience is valid or real no matter what the measurable results in terms of human behaviour. Ironically, all activity based on the ego, by operating in a very limited, practical, self-seeking manner is considered perfectly rational and comprehensible. At this limited level of being, action calls forth reaction in a mechanical, unconscious way. This accounts for most of human conduct. The intractable problems that face mankind, however, can rarely be resolved at this level of consciousness. The reconciling principle that creates resolution, can't take hold without accessing a higher level of consciousness. Intention, determination and goodwill are not sufficient to make this happen. Only 'spiritual intelligence' arising from transcendence of the ego, can accomplish it. Spiritual teacher, Eckhart Tolle, describes this as follows:

> The ego may be clever, but it is not intelligent. Cleverness pursues its own little aims. Intelligence sees the larger whole in which all things are connected. Cleverness is motivated by self-interest, and it is extremely short-sighted. Most politicians and businesspeople are clever. Very few are intelligent. Whatever is attained through cleverness is short-lived and always turns out to be eventually self-defeating. **Cleverness divides, intelligence includes.**[2]

Eternity will not be long enough to resolve the Israeli / Palestinian conflict without some participant bringing this quality of intelligence to bear on the issue. This was Mandela's legacy in South Africa, that of Mahatma Gandhi in India, Aung San Su Kyi in Burma and Vaclav Havel in Czechoslovakia. By lowering the Iron Curtain, Gorbachev also proved himself to be no ordinary politician. What distinguishes these men from able and competent politicians in general, is an 'intelligence' that cannot be defined in ordinary terms. Although often denounced as too abstract to have relevance to the affairs of the real world, the effects of an intelligence integrating spirituality are nevertheless profound, long lasting and very, very real. These men, and others like them, have demonstrated this beyond any reasonable doubt. The difficulties in the world created by the self-limiting consciousness of the ego can only be resolved by rising above it. Einstein would seem to be suggesting the same thing when he stated that 'the problems that exist in the world cannot be solved by the level of thinking that created them.' Identification with ego has dominated our history but has now reached its limits as the driving force of life. Failure to recognise this fact will provoke grave disorders in the future that can eventually threaten our survival.

IV

As an example of the extent to which the ego can cause havoc throughout the world, let us focus for a moment on the events surrounding the financial services industry in the United States in 2008. In a paroxysm of greed, 'brilliant' young men, sitting in front of computer screens, devised obscure investment instruments that routinely produced enormous profits for the industry. We all woke up one morning to discover that traditional banking, a staid, unglamorous but vital service to society, had somehow transformed itself into a modern day El Dorado. When the sub-prime problems came to a head, the industry was suddenly threatened with collapse and, with it, the financial stability of the world.

Even as this precipitated the severest world recession since the Great Depression of the 1930's, with public funds having to come to the rescue of the banking sector, the members of that community saw fit to award themselves $123 billion in bonuses for the year 2008 when these events occurred. In what way did Wall Street react to the resulting opprobrium? The following year, without a hint of contrition, they announced an all-time record in bonuses of $145 billion! It defies belief. Having contracted chronic losses due to the sub-prime meltdown, where did the money come from to do this? Instead of distributing the federal T.A.R.P (Troubled Assets Relief Program) money designed to extend credit to the nation, the banking community used these funds for speculative purposes to boost their earnings. On the basis of these 'stolen' earnings, enormous bonuses were again distributed, this time at the very moment that the foreclosure rates in the US were breaking all records, causing ruin and suffering to millions. This situation happened in all Western countries, particularly in the UK, where the banking sector went into meltdown. Furthermore, the wild stampede to acquire riches on Wall Street and in London not only drained American and British societies of some of their best brains, but also saw the proportion of GNP attributable to the financial sector in the U.S rise from 12% to 40% without producing a single item of functional use to society! It is of interest to note that Nobel laureate Economist, James Tobin, made the following comments in 1984, twenty-four years before the recent debacle:

> We are throwing more and more of our resources, including the cream of our youth, into financial activities remote from the production of goods and services, into activities that generate high private rewards disproportionate to their social productivity.[3]

In the meantime, farmers and manufacturers of goods most vitally needed by society, along with much of the American and British middle class, have seen their standards of living moderate for years. Nurses, policeman and firemen, all of whom save lives on a daily basis, and in the case of policemen and firemen, risk their own, are very modestly compensated for their indispensable services to society. Even without bonuses the mean annual salary for a securities industry employee was just under $400,000, ten times more than the average US or British worker. Aberration is too mild a word to describe these developments. This can only be seen as the most significant departure from sanity and good sense that modern society has ever experienced. Grotesque as it is, it is important to understand that this had been going on for years, as James Tobin's comments above indicate, without it being considered abnormal. Only when the financial house of cards threatened to collapse, did this folly become unacceptable in the eyes of the world. Although governments in Europe have reacted by trying to cap or tax these windfalls, there is nothing to indicate that the sense of entitlement of the members of the financial community has in any way diminished.

I mention this only to show how inured we have become to the pathological level of selfishness in our midst. For years, the perpetrators of the biggest hold-up in history were referred to, with a mixture of envy and admiration, as golden boys! Let us not forget that greed on Wall Street was satirised in the form of Gordon (Greed is Good) Gekko in the Oliver Stone film 'Wall Street' no less than twenty-three years ago. Gekko and his clones, however, are not only alive and well but also thriving as never before. To be fair this is not just an American phenomenon. The very same thing applies to the United Kingdom and to some extent everywhere. Nevertheless, a year after the near collapse of the financial system, Wall Street, as we have seen, is quite unrepentant and is fighting tooth and claw to maintain its unjustifiable privileges. One has to wonder to what dark cavern of our beings has been relegated the virtue of self-restraint or the feeling of shame? What function, if any, does conscience have in the world today?

The explanation, I believe, lies in the absence of a certain quality of education. It is deeply dispiriting to see how young children, such fertile terrain for spiritual nourishment, slowly lose their 'openness' to that reality by following the example of their parents. A transmission of 'unawareness' that we all share is then unwittingly set in place, which over time has fashioned the nature of our culture and society. An incalculable amount of human potential is squandered in this way. In the meantime, devoted and well-intentioned parents continue to sacrifice all to give their children an education that they are unable to identify as being incomplete. We spend many years at school learning mathematics, history, biology, physics and chemistry, but have never been taught the rudiments of the Perennial Philosophy. 'Self-knowledge' is a complete abstraction for most people, along with any concept of the purpose of life beyond being successful — without that being defined in any terms other than self-aggrandisement.

In one sense, 'higher education' is clearly a misnomer. Advanced levels of education, by accumulating greater knowledge in ever more specialised fields, tend to increase rather than diminish the fragmented way in which we view the world. We are then left highly prepared and informed to do little more than advance our self-interest in a manner that more and more people experience as humanly unfulfilling. The frantic pursuit of distractions and amusements of every variety can never obscure this fact from us entirely. Try as we might, we can't escape the fact that only by evaluating and relating learning in terms of the meaning and purpose of life, can knowledge be of any psychological value to us. Learning to 'be' must surely take precedence over knowing how to 'do', the former determining the latter. Otherwise, in spite of an unprecedented advance in learning and the unlimited availability of information, people seem to have less and less understanding as to what gives real meaning to their personal lives or to society as a whole. There is evidence of this at all socio-economic levels.

It is this fundamental confusion, as to means and ends that renders intelligent and educated men and women shallow, and has virtually banished the word wisdom from our vocabulary. Lip service is paid to religion, of course, but very few take Christ's teaching seriously when it conflicts with everyday pragmatism. Take a phrase from the Bible like 'the kingdom of heaven is within you' (Luke: 17.21). Who would suspect that it is a piece of practical psychological advice of enormous value? Similarly, we are told in the Bible that 'love of money is the root of all evil' (1. Timothy: 6.10). Most people enthusiastically agree but spend their entire lives trying to make as much of it as possible! The Bible also suggests we be 'as little children' (Matthew: 18.3) which is to say, open, truthful and sincere in all our doings. Again, while there is very little disagreement with this in principle, it is virtually non-existent in practice. And so it goes.

The Idiot by Dostoyevsky, one of the greatest novels ever written, has an important relevance to this question. The book is about a marginal, semi-mystical Russian aristocrat called Prince Myshkin. Because he lacks the conventional forms of guile and artifice expected of someone of his social rank, and relates to others with complete sincerity, St Petersburg society treats him like an idiot. As the story develops, however, we discover that far from being simple or foolish, Myshkin, in his guileless manner, proves himself to be deep and perspicacious. His interaction over time with the 'clever' people, who had treated him with condescension, gradually exposes their futile and shallow ways. In the unfolding of this long and complex story, Dostoyevsky shows us that possessing biblical qualities of modesty, truthfulness and sincerity, entirely misread by a society dedicated to superficiality, is by no means the handicap in life one might assume.

This has huge relevance to us today. The world is awash with 'clever' people who stand at the pinnacle of society, control many important aspects of our lives, but who, in spite of being savvy and having apparent effectiveness in the world, are often empty, shallow and insecure. Technocratic competence, capable, realistic and free of moral aspiration, has become the paradigm of our time. Politicians and corporate leaders, with few exceptions, typify this mold and are totally unequipped to instill a more evolved vision of human possibilities that is so urgently required at this time. What's worse, we don't expect it of them because we don't know what it is!

As a result, all we see at the G7 and G20 inter-governmental meetings on regulating international finance or climate change are measures devoid of creative inspiration. Worthy objectives are constantly being announced, though concerted action is very rare. There is a very good reason for this. We cannot be moved to make the radical changes required of us at this late hour, without change being understood in far wider spiritual terms. While shortsighted pragmatism prevails, we seem to stumble from crisis to crisis fighting the last war, incapable, or better, unwilling to identify the new adversary. The Copenhagen Conference on Climate Change in late 2009 was the most recent example of this collective failure. Negotiations stalled, as they always do, when nations are unable to rise above an exclusively pragmatic view of what constitutes their interests.

Approached from a spiritual perspective, the notion of 'self-interest' can modify itself rapidly. This would open the way to altogether new forms of mutual help and co-operation. There really is no other way we can tackle this massive challenge. As it is, we run the risk that 'immobilisation' will install itself until it is too late to take effective action. Clearly, an entirely new impetus is needed, but where is it to come from? At this crucial juncture, we must be brought to the understanding that the origin of the problems of the world *lies in our spiritually impoverished conception of life*. It is inescapable that the central problems of mankind derive from this 'inconvenient truth'. Addressing the superficial consequences alone, as we do repeatedly, changes nothing. It's like bailing water out of a sinking boat without trying to repair the leak. Moreover, if we are under the illusion that all this will take care of itself with time, it is highly instructive to read the following impressions of Dorothy Sayers, one of the most respected commentators on modern society, written back in 1954:

> And since we are today well convinced that society is in a bad way and not necessarily evolving in the direction of perfectibility, we find it easy enough to recognise the various stages by which the deep of corruption is reached; Futility, lack of faith, the drift into loose morality, greedy consumption, financial irresponsibility, a self-opinionated and obstinate individualism, violence, sterility, and lack of reverence

for life and property including one's own, the exploitation of sex, the debasing of language by advertisement and propaganda, the commercialising of religion, the pandering to superstition and the conditioning of people's minds by mass hysteria and sensationalism of all kinds, venality and string-pulling in public affairs, hypocrisy, dishonesty in material things, intellectual dishonesty, the fomenting of discord (class against class, nation against nation) for what one can get out of it, the exploitation of the lowest and most stupid of mass-emotions….these are the all-too-recognisable stages that lead to the cold death of society and the extinguishing of all civilised relations.[4]

Few can still believe that we are on the right path and that the problems of society that Dorothy Sayers described almost sixty years ago, identical to our own today, can now be resolved by methods inherent to the same vision of life. It should be clear by now that these problems are not the result of economic mismanagement or misguided policies on the right or left of the political spectrum. They are merely the symptoms on the outside of a moral and spiritual void that is destroying us from the inside. It is not surprising, therefore, to discover that the world of politics and politicians, with few exceptions, is a spectacle of extraordinary mediocrity. Accustomed as we are to seeing the most abject of human failings routinely exemplified by tyrants and dictators across the world, you don't have to go to extremes such as Kim Jong II, Mugabe or even Vladimir Putin, to know this. It is not uncommon to see the men and women who guide the destinies of nations in our more respectable western democracies, behave in vain, conniving, dishonest, immature and capricious ways. George W. Bush's justification for invading Iraq was a well-documented hoax of historic proportions. With the theatrics of his 'mission accomplished' speech on board an aircraft carrier, when the war had hardly begun, he achieved unmatched heights of foolishness in the eyes of the world. A few years later, a thoroughly scurrilous campaign of disinformation and media manipulation enabled him to be decisively re-elected to a second term in office. As hard to comprehend as this may be, even to many Americans, this was not happening in an emerging nation, but in the world's most powerful and admired democracy. By the same token, Bill Clinton, a likeable sexual rogue before and during his time in office, lied, squirmed and dissimulated when questioned about his 'peccadilloes' in office at a Senate hearing. Cornered by the evidence, the leader of the western world finally owned up to his 'lack of good judgment'! Again, one has to be reminded that it was the President of the United States being questioned in the Senate, not a mischievous schoolboy caught out in some prank. You would think that the debasement of the venerable and august office of the President in this humiliating manner would be a traumatic experience for a nation aspiring to be an example to others. What happened as a result? Due to America's diminished capacity to envisage, let alone, demand great qualities from its leaders at the time, the Clinton presidency was succeeded by that of George W. Bush under the most dubious of electoral circumstances. His two terms in office were then to be the darkest era in modern political history.

The record of Britain's recent leaders is hardly better. Tony Blair slavishly followed George W. Bush into the Iraq War, and his successor, Gordon Brown, has overseen the collapse of the economy, to leave a country mired in debt. How is it that sensible and educated people in western democracies, after prolonged scrutiny of the candidates, routinely choose as their highest representatives to the most demanding jobs on earth, men and women of such mediocre moral calibre? How can it be explained, for example, that Silvio Berlusconi, former crooner with a questionable ascent to riches, heading up a media empire that has a virtual monopoly in Italy, has been elected to office twice by one of the most educated and sophisticated electorates in the world? This unstoppable septuagenarian with the resilience of a gladiator managed to navigate between a sleazy sex scandal, accusations of ties with the mob, incessant gaffes and an economy on life-support to hold the confidence of a large segment of the Italian nation. It is truly dismaying. The only possible explanation lies in the fact that electorates in general, which is to say, all of us, are not 'awake'.

Where there is no spiritual awareness, there is no depth to our insights or to our expectations. There is nothing within us capable of resisting the kind of shallow manipulation of our sentiments and beliefs that allows these things to happen. The ancient and sacred instinct for 'sensing' the deeper significance of things, once characteristic of many traditional societies, has long gone. Again, this is perfectly exemplified in the case of Bill Clinton. Even before the Monica Lewinsky affair it was generally accepted that Clinton had a flawed character. The success of his presidency was later judged on the basis of his undoubted intelligence and abilities that somehow became separated in people's minds from his moral character. The fact that integrity is indivisible and applies to the whole man or it doesn't apply at all, no longer seemed to matter. Provided the collective interests of the US were being promoted successfully, as was the case during the Clinton presidency, all other considerations became irrelevant. When Vaclav Havel once said, 'I favour politics as practical morality, as service to the truth …and humanly measured care for our fellow man,' you have to wonder what universe of men and women he was addressing.

In the universe most of us are familiar with, high ideals and a moral instinct can only be seen as an obstacle to success. Governments worldwide regularly cave in to the pressure of expedience when it comes to dealing with nations who abuse human rights or possess valuable resources. The craven way governments behave with respect to the question of Tibet has become a shameful spectacle throughout the world. To avoid antagonising China, the Dalai Lama is routinely ushered in through back doors to meet with minor government officials with limited media coverage. The world has entirely reneged on its moral responsibility to defend a defenseless nation. Some major contracts would no doubt be at risk if this were to happen, but so is the moral integrity of the international community. Compromise after compromise is being made to safeguard personal and national 'interests' in this way. What we don't seem to understand is that this type of 'realism', applied now to everything, comes with a cost far greater than those 'interests' could ever represent. The financial meltdown of 2008 should be proof enough that greed and selfishness, the consequence of such a narrow and self-centred vision of life, is already the cause of economic instability and social injustice in our societies. The millions of people who have lost their homes as a result of the sub-prime debacle can readily testify to that fact. Machines will one day be able to make competent, rational decisions for us but they will never be capable of wisdom or moral reasoning. More than anything else, isn't this what we should expect from the men and women who we elect to govern us? Shouldn't we expect this of ourselves?

Our failure to understand that corporate or political leadership can only operate to the benefit of society when it is founded on this form of moral integrity, holds little promise for the future. From the simplest to the highest tasks, all human activities are branches of this same tree. There can be no enduring stability to our institutions or our individual lives without this. The following passage from academic, cultural critic and farmer, Wendell Berry, has particular relevance to this question:

> Several years ago I discussed with a friend of mine that we might make money by marketing some inferior lambs. My friend thought for a minute and then he said, 'I'm in the business of producing good lambs and I am not going to sell any other kind'. He also said that he kept the weeds out of his crops for the same reason that he washed his face. The human race has survived by that attitude. It can **only** survive by that attitude… Such an attitude does not come from education. It does not even come from principle. It comes from a passion that is culturally prepared, a passion for excellence and order that is handed down to young people by older people whom they respect and love. **When we destroy the possibility of that succession we will have gone far towards destroying ourselves.**

Where do we now stand in relationship to such wise counsel? One is obliged to recognise that the 'succession' Wendell Berry describes is a relic of the past. Those who take pride in a job well done for its own sake, and not just for profit or publicity, are an endangered species.

The highest reward for the least application of time, effort, and responsibility is the rule rather than the exception these days. This is the meaning behind the distasteful slogan 'time is money' that most people in business are obliged to respect. In the autumn of 2008 the economic foundations of the world were severely shaken and the world stared chaos in the face. On a smaller scale, but for much the same reasons, this has happened no less than four times in the last thirty years, notably with the Japanese property bubble and the US Savings and Loan Crisis of the 1980's, the 1997 Asian Financial Crisis, and the frenzied dot.com bubble of 2000-2001.

In the recent crisis, disaster was averted by the un-precedented measures taken by government central bankers worldwide, but the same danger persists because nothing has changed in the fundamental attitudes of society. It's a virtual certainty, therefore, that it will happen again. Even the large bonuses on Wall Street and London, so symbolic of the imbalances and excesses that precipitated the problems, have not been reigned in. If we can agree that integrity founded on the traditional values referred to by Wendell Berry is the only force capable of binding together the intricate strands of global political, social and economic inter-dependence, what are we to expect in the future? The market-based system of free enterprise is dependent on strict regulations and the confidence of investors. The destructive forces of greed and unbridled self-interest are a constant threat to the whole capitalist system. The world coming within a hairsbreadth of total chaos doesn't seem to have served as sufficient warning.

The spiritual deterioration we see today has also given rise to the incremental acceptance of ever-lower moral expectations with regard to human behaviour in general. 'Relativism' and the growing embrace of 'tolerance,' are nothing but the fashionable intellectual rationalizations of our diminished capacity to have well-founded convictions. 'Weakness of attitude becomes weakness of character', said Einstein. As this spiritual hollow deepens, incoherence and dysfunction manifest themselves around us in ever more disturbing ways. Outer collapse is the logical consequence and reflection of inner collapse. The word 'civilisation' acquires its meaning from the spiritual and aesthetic accomplishments of mankind. When the material outpaces the spiritual, as is the case today, the notion of 'progress' becomes a travesty. The present particularity, however, is that for the first time in history our civilisation is being threatened not only from its internal contradictions but also, on account of the deteriorating state of the planet, from the outside also. How far are we from the danger point? It's hard to say but the portents are mounting. W. B. Yeats, the great Irish poet, wrote in *The Second Coming* that 'things fall apart; the centre doesn't hold...the best lack all conviction. While the worst are full of passionate intensity.' Although written in 1919, the poem in its entirety draws an astonishingly accurate sketch of the world today.

V

An alarming divergence exists between the arbitrary and opportunistic use of human intelligence and ingenuity on the one hand and wisdom on the other. This gap, widening by the day, is one of the most striking characteristics of the world today. New technologies tumble out of the minds of the young geniuses in Silicon Valley and other places without an understanding of the effects they may have on our lives beyond their perceived 'usefulness'. In the past few decades, an endless array of technological gadgets has been creeping into our lives in this way.

Improvement follows on improvement, so that now we can receive and send e-mails on our mobile phones, check stock prices, watch the news and so on. In Japan you can even find a small gadget attached to your reading glasses that can play a DVD allowing you to watch movies at all times, even when walking! With fifty per cent of the world's population living on two dollars a day, is this really where our ingenuity and resources are being put to best use? I mean, aren't we breaking new ground in all that is spurious and superfluous in technology? Hasn't 'our technology exceeded our humanity', as Einstein put it? If market forces are responsible for this kind of absurdity then clearly supply and demand are not responsive to good sense. In no time at all, we find that we don't live in the same world as we did as little as a generation ago. We have all now been conditioned to embrace the world of information technology. Whether we are aware of it or not, the unlimited opportunity for interactivity and communication via the Internet has surreptitiously introduced a virtual dimension to our lives that never existed before. Through the use of blogs, Facebook, My Space and so on, we communicate with each other to an unprecedented degree. The continuous but largely inconsequential nature of this interactivity, however, is causing creative introspection and the use of the imagination to take a back seat in our lives. 'The medium is the message', Marshall McLuhan presciently announced in the 1960's. This is the case today to a far greater extent than in his time. On the other hand, the imaginative exuberance and creative eccentricity of that era is in short supply.

The Internet is unquestionably a revolutionary means of communication and the most extensive source of information known to man. It's understandable, therefore, that its contribution to our lives goes unquestioned. Useful as it is, one is also obliged to recognise that the advent of all this technology has occasioned some collateral damage. We have adapted to the new reality so rapidly that this fact seems to pass unnoticed. In no time at all we have seen the great works of literature, the kind that have animated hearts and souls for hundreds of years, relegated to the musty bookshelves of libraries, where they remain largely unread. In the process, however, a whole sensibility has altered. Allan Bloom, former Professor of Social Thought at the University of Chicago had this to say on the subject:

> It is not merely tradition that is lost when the voice of civilisation elaborated over millennia has been stilled in this way. It is 'being' itself that vanishes... deprived of literary guidance, (the young) no longer have any image of a perfect soul and hence do not long to have one. They do not even imagine that there is such a thing.[5]

It can be argued that these developments are all part of the normal evolution of society and that the values of great literature are no longer relevant to our image-based world of rapid communication. Given the direction things have taken, it was no doubt unavoidable. But what we have to ask ourselves is this. What should come first, is it the human being, possessor of a soul and the spiritual requirements that come with it unchanged over thousands of years, or is it technology, the child of human ingenuity, that has created its own requirements outside the timeless reality of who we are? Communication has become a series of word and sound bites on Facebook, e-mails, blogs and mobile phones. There is no doubt, however, that a person's whole subjective world operates differently under these conditions. An uninspiring, prosaic, matter-of-fact objectivity has replaced a richer subjective world, romanticism and a certain kind of innocence. Saul Bellow, winner of the Nobel Prize for

Literature in 1976 and an astute observer of the ways of the world, described the situation in this way:

> The power to experience is taken from us by our lack of cultural development so that **we don't know how to interpret experience**. If you ask people to explain why they are what they are, why they do what they do, they are on the moon when they try to explain... **Culture means having access to your soul.**[6]

A dreary pragmatism seems to have descended on a world that has lost touch with its divinity. People have more of everything but most of us have the distinct impression that the quality of life diminishes by the day. Why is this? There is no obvious explanation other than to acknowledge that assessing 'quality' is a matter for the spirit, not the mind alone. The essential difference between Leo Tolstoy and a respected modern author, for example, is not their respective talents as writers *but the spiritual urge underlying the creative process*. There is no valid way to replicate these things. We construct our own vision and understanding on the backs of those who preceded us. The passing on of this accumulated wisdom is tradition in its most meaningful sense. When this chain of transmission is broken we are 'lost in the cosmos', as Walker Percy put it. Our ability to identify 'quality', the fruit of that transmission, is then lost. In strictly material terms and from the ego's standpoint, technological progress is a powerful contributor to personal fulfilment.

In spiritual terms, however, you can't dissociate happiness from a certain kind of simplicity independent of material enhancement. Much confusion and despair arises from the absence of a proper understanding of this fact. You don't have to be a trained psychologist to see that with alarming levels of violence, delinquency, sexual dysfunction, depression, alcohol and drug abuse, the conventional prescriptions for happiness are not working and the human psyche is under extreme duress. Our era of technological abundance is clearly not delivering on its promise.

VI

There is little doubt, therefore, that the paramount challenges of our time are psychological rather than material in nature. Pathologies and anomalies resulting from this are now commonplace. For example, why do so many people who have 'succeeded' in life, who have wealth, power and prestige, still experience personal insecurity? It was recently published in the *International Herald Tribune* that people in general were more willing to accept a lower level of salary provided others were earning less, rather than double the amount if others earned more. What is the explanation for such insecurity? The answer is that we can send a man to the moon and invent the Internet, but the basic mechanism of what makes people happy and psychologically secure remains a mystery to them.

The result for most people (and in a more concentrated form among the wealthy) is that life is often accompanied by an indefinable sensation of anxiety. This is the human condition referred to by Sakyamuni Buddha 2500 years ago when, in his First Noble Truth, he stated that life is suffering. Although few people would readily acknowledge this fact under normal conditions of life in the West, the habitual response is to shore up their lives with material goods in the belief that this will make them secure and happy. The fact that both these goals remain elusive only seems to spur them further along the same path.

As we fill our lives with activity and ever more elaborate distractions, the sensation of emptiness recedes but never entirely disappears. In fact, the existential discomforts that linger on, gave rise some years ago to a body of literature by such eminent European writers as Jean-Paul Sartre and Albert Camus that amounted to nothing much more than the intellectual glorification of the absurdity and incoherence of life. Although this would not seem very compelling or inspiring in itself, books like *The Stranger* by Albert Camus became the cult favourite of generations of young people, who, untouched by the great mystical teachings, continue to suffer from the feeling that life has no meaning. Alcohol abuse and other self-destructive habits on the rise among the young would seem to reflect this state of anxiety and disenchantment. The ever-higher rates of depression and suicide are further evidence that our psychic health has deteriorated dramatically, even as the level of prosperity in all industrial societies has multiplied itself in the last fifty years.

Humanity has been blessed with the gift of consciousness as a means of discovering its divine nature. Contrary to the conventional view, experiencing this precious birthright is the only source of real meaning in life. Everything else is secondary. When William Blake said that, 'each man is haunted until his humanity awakens', he was referring to the discomfort experienced at the core of our beings when this fact is overlooked. Owing to the tyranny of the ego, this is the lot of the vast majority of people. After centuries of struggle and deprivation, we finally climbed out of poverty in the West and acquired unprecedented wealth, only to discover that happiness was still an elusive factor in our lives. What went wrong? Aren't we supposed to be the fortunate beneficiaries of the highest standards of living in the history of mankind? Hasn't everything imaginable been done to facilitate our lives? Now that we have mobile phones, air-conditioned malls, spotless supermarkets, fast food at every corner, cars with multiple gadgets and manicured suburban developments with clean, tidy homes, what is the missing ingredient? The answer is that in the same way that a plant cannot grow without light, we cannot experience plenitude without living in accordance with our spiritual nature. 'Man wishes to be happy even when he so lives as makes happiness impossible,' said St Augustine. To experience happiness, we don't need to deplete the resources of the planet so as to have our lives facilitated to the unnecessary degree that is the case today in the West. Our dependence on the superfluous is an addiction of a pathological order. The sensation of 'dissatisfaction' will stalk us for as long as we fail to see that material satiety, notably at the cost of perpetuating a radically unequal distribution of resources in the world, will never provide us with the contentment we seek.

VII

Another area of life that demonstrates the breakdown in the organic relationship that we have with nature is the question of how and what we eat. At the dawn of the 21st century one of the greatest threats to life is not terrorism or nuclear extinction but what we put in our mouths. Time-honoured rituals and habits of finding nourishment from eating wholesome food have been replaced in modern times by the industrial processing of food, fast food, fast (microwave) cooking, genetically modified food, food irradiation, and the near disappearance of regular traditional family meals. Subjecting the food we eat to the imperatives of commerce has been one of the most lethal developments since the splitting of the atom. With a disregard for public health of surreal dimensions, the food and beverage industry is single-handedly responsible for the current epidemic of obesity and diabetes in the US, in particular, but spreading fast to Europe and elsewhere. Sugar, salt, trans fats and all manner of food additives and preservatives have been introduced into every morsel of processed food we eat. The Standard American Diet (SAD) fully deserves its acronym! Add to this the prolif-eration of soft drinks, cookies, sweets, cereals, candies and sweet food in general and you have the prescription for the breakdown of public health on the massive scale we witness today. It is beyond comprehension that the most informed and educated societies in the history of the world display such ignorance when it comes to the food they eat.

Second in line of responsibility comes the pharmaceutical industry which, again, for reasons of profit, continues to purvey the false message that common degenerative diseases such as high blood pressure, arthritis, and cardio-vascular problems in general, are the natural outcome of ageing and should be treated by taking pharmaceutical medication. They have been so successful in disseminating this inaccurate message, that products designed exclusively to alleviate symptoms, (often with serious side-effects), but fail to address the original causes of disease, sell in hundreds of billions of dollars annually. The fact that these diseases arise primarily from our chronic eating habits and can be prevented by eating the right foods, as is the case in many parts of the world where different eating habits exist, is roundly dismissed by so-called experts, usually from the industry itself! Prevention by natural means is, of course, unprofitable. Unfortunately, the medical establishment is also involved in this conspiracy, as medical doctors have relatively little knowledge of nutrition and are trained in the use of pharmaceutical products almost exclusively. As a result, the highly persuasive evidence that certain dietary habits combined with the quality of the food we eat can effectively prevent disease never gets the attention it deserves. It is hard to imagine a comparable act of collective amnesia. We would do well to heed the words of Herophilus (300 B.C.): 'When health is absent, wisdom cannot reveal itself, art cannot become manifest, strength cannot be exerted, wealth is useless, reason is powerless'.

The question of health and the ignorance that surrounds it is yet another example of the incoherence in our lives resulting from our inability to see life and our physical health as a spiritual 'whole'. In the process of modernisation we have managed to separate body and soul in the mistaken belief that each has separate and distinct requirements. We now consider it perfectly normal to work all day sitting in an enclosed space in front of a screen, maintain health and fitness by 'working out' on machines in another enclosed space, eat ready-made meals supplemented by vitamins to assure nutrition, and watch films, read books or go to the opera to address the needs of mind and spirit. It is rarely suspected in this practical organisation of our activities that the body and soul operate through the *natural inter-dependence* of these functions and that such fragmentation is harmful to both body and soul. This was common knowledge to the 'primitive' and aboriginal peoples that preceded us, to whom all forms of activity were enacted as a single, sacred ritual of life. It is almost certain that the psychic disorders common to our 'civilised' societies were entirely foreign to them. Likewise, we fail to recognise the fact, once again self-evident to traditional societies, that we are a figment of nature and that our physical health is dependent on the rich, natural offerings of the soil, uncontaminated, unrefined and unmodified by human intervention for the purposes of commerce. Food as a life source is sacred and has often been viewed as such by past civilisations. In our reckless disregard of our environment and to our infinite peril, it is probable at this point that we have managed to defile our only source of sustenance in an irreversible manner.

If we were to single out a single measure that would have social, moral, ecological, and economic consequences of unimaginable proportions in the world, it would be to cease or substantially reduce the consumption of meat. In the first place, humans are not carnivores by nature. The human colon is long, like that of grass-eating horses or cows, rather than short, like flesh-eating lions and tigers. A cat, for example, secretes ten times the amount of hydrochloric acid for digestive purposes than we do. It should come as no surprise, therefore, to discover that meat eating is harmful to our health. The incidence of cardio-vascular disease, arthritis, certain cancers and osteoporosis are demonstrably and causally linked to the consumption of animal protein and fats. The annual cost of treating these diseases runs into the hundreds of billions of dollars, which amount could alone eradicate extreme poverty and malnutrition in the world. 'Nothing will benefit human health and increase chances of survival for life on earth as much as the evolution to a vegetarian diet,' said Einstein. In itself, the grain used to fatten livestock in the US could feed five times its population. It is astonishing to discover, furthermore, that it takes an average 2500 gallons of water, the most precious resource on the planet, *to produce a single pound of meat.* 'The water that goes into a thousand pound steer could float a destroyer,' announced *Newsweek* in 1981. Water is far scarcer today.

With regards to ecology, the situation is even more dramatic. Dr Harold Bernard, an agricultural expert with the US Environmental Protection Agency stated that the runoff of liquid and solid wastes from the millions of animals on the 206,000 feedlots in the US 'are ten to several hundred times more concentrated than raw domestic sewage'. It was reported that in Omaha, Nebraska alone, for example, 100,000 pounds of slaughterhouse sewage spews into the sewage system and from there into the Missouri River *each* day. The ecological consequences do not end there, however. We have depleted our topsoil and decimated forests all over the world for grazing purposes. This has greatly reduced the capacity of the planet to absorb carbon dioxide. Cattle breeding, through the production of methane, is now responsible for fully twenty percent of greenhouse gasses going into the atmosphere. It is dismaying to discover that this even exceeds emissions from the transport sector.

Finally, the most important consequence is undoubtedly the cessation of the unspeakable cruelty inflicted on animals in the industrial production of meat and poultry. 'While we ourselves are the living graves of murdered beasts, how can we expect any ideal conditions on this earth?' said George Bernard Shaw. For entirely selfish reasons we pamper our domestic pets, are attentive to their every need and weep at their disappearance, at the same time as we eat the flesh of other animals that have been subjected to conditions of extreme cruelty without giving them a thought. It is impossible to estimate the moral harm we inflict upon ourselves by this abominable disregard of animals. Although 'custom will reconcile people to any atrocity', as George Bernard Shaw said, surely it's time to modify this morally indefensible habit so as to improve our health, arrest the ecological damage to the Earth, liberate funds to alleviate poverty, save water, reduce greenhouse gasses and be compassionate to all living creatures *all at one time*. I leave the last word on this subject to Jesus Himself (from the Essene Gospel of Peace):

> And the flesh of slain beasts in his body will become his own tomb. For I tell you, he who kills, kills himself, and whoso eats the flesh of slain beasts eats the body of death.

VIII

In the meantime, how has all this 'unconsciousness' played out in the world at large? The financial crisis that originated in the United States in 2008 spread like a virus throughout the planet causing a precipitous drop in demand from frightened and over-indebted consumers. This, as I have already mentioned, left all governments strangely bewildered and at a loss. The reflex reaction was to infuse gigantic sums of money (fabricated from nowhere) into the economic machine in the hope of stimulating demand. It seems that the survival of the capitalist system hinges once again on the resuscitation of our collective urge to spend money on goods and services we can no longer afford or need. As the poet Wordsworth said, 'getting and spending, we lay waste our powers'. The truth of these words is undeniable. We seem to bestride the planet like clumsy giants in varying states of moral con-fusion, psychological frailty and insecurity. As an antidote, we have subsequently tended to borrow money in ever greater quantities. The widespread use of credit has always meant that we consume today what we shall earn tomorrow. As this takes for granted a smooth and sustained course of economic expansion, it is a very risky habit. The slightest reversal, as we have seen recently, instantly creates a negative spiral in the opposite direction.

For this reason, it is generally agreed that it is salutary for people to be content with what they have and only pay for what they can afford. Given the way our system works, however, this is no longer an option. At this point only the continuation of habits manifestly harmful to the planet and us can keep capitalism on course, and every government in the world hangs its hopes on just such an outcome. This state of affairs is not only incoherent and perverse but also totally irresponsible. 'The idea that you can solve a problem of too much debt and too much consumption with more debt and more consumption is beyond belief', commented financier Jim Rogers. By being dependent on growth at all cost, our capitalist system has finally run ahead of itself in an unsustainable manner and revealed its limits. How can one hope to reduce CO_2 emissions, reverse the depletion of finite resources, restore ecological balance to the environment at the same time as we maintain living standards in the West at present levels — all this, while creating similar opportunities in the rapidly emerging countries of the world, all of which aspire with great determination to what we have. It is now an accepted scientific conclusion that if everybody were living and consuming as we do in the West, we would need three additional planets to support us. How on earth do we reconcile this fact with the reality of the one exhausted planet that we do have? Furthermore, all this must happen in a context where world population is estimated to grow to nine billion within forty years. *It simply can't be done* and the sooner our politicians, economists and 'experts' acknowledge this evident fact, the sooner mankind will be obliged to envisage an alternative way of living and being. It's our only hope. What alternatives do we have?

When our Indian Professor at Davos suggested that we should all aspire to lives of elegant simplicity, one can only imagine that he was referring to a major adjustment in our material expectations in the West, so as to accommodate a higher standard of living in the emerging nations of the world. To 'live simply so that others can simply live', as Gandhi urged, would not be just a material adjustment, but also a spiritual one of great significance. Contrary to the conventional view and for the reasons we have outlined earlier, it is reasonable to expect that a lower standard of living in a material sense can also be accompanied by a higher standard of contentment in a spiritual one. Economist E. F. Schumacher described this unconventional logic in terms of the Buddhist view of economics:

> The keynote is simplicity and non-violence. From an economist's point of view, the marvel of the Buddhist way of life is the utter rationality of its pattern — **amazingly small means leading to extraordinarily satisfactory results. Buddhists sees the essence of civilisation not in multiplication of wants, but in the purification of human character.**[7]

After all, where has the opposite logic taken us? Having gone to the limits of 'more,' can't we now explore the nature of 'less'? Selfishness or its more acceptable version, self-interest, is exclusively at the service of the urge to have or be more. If we were to reverse this logic and experiment with less, egoism would inevitably diminish. Envy, pride and vanity bred of the inherent insecurities of an egoistic vision of life, would also naturally decrease. The ego, the greatest imposter of all, would finally have lost its *raison d'être*. If this sounds preposterous, it does so only because we have become so numb and de-sensitized to the incoherence of our ways. Why should we believe that our self-centred and destructive manner of living is ineluctable? Why are we so convinced that our potential for 'love', in the highest sense of the word, cannot be realised? After all, it is not a complete abstraction. We have seen it manifested on rare occasions in the world, Mother Theresa and the Dalai Lama spring to mind, but there are countless other lesser known examples. It is even possible that we have had a fleeting experience of it in our own lives. Why should we resign ourselves to the notion that we are inherently egoistic and that no such potential exists for us? The human capacity for self-transcendence and spiritual evolution has been the unchanging message of all mystical teachings from time immemorial. What we are now, we are told, forever holds within itself the possibility of what we can become. The Human Potential Movement is based on this truth. Looked at from a less abstract angle, it could be described as an evolution towards 'positive' selfishness, a sensible and practical way to be happy without it being harmful to ourselves, others and our natural environment, as the Buddhists envisage.

For this, the mystical teachings are like how-to instruction manuals. Their aim has always been to guide us away from the egoistic mirage that passes for reality towards our veritable nature and the fruits of this birthright. But in order to better understand their message, all prior ideas concerning 'religion' should be set aside. The conventional notions of 'morality' arise from the fact that we live selfishly, due to egoistic habits, but are bound by religious tradition to certain rules of conduct, telling us that we should live differently. The tug of war between the two creates a psychological tension that we experience as 'guilt'. Religion is then associated in the minds of many with something forbidding and austere that somehow prevents us from enjoying the pleasures of life. Although nothing could be further from the truth, such, for the most part, is how our Christian heritage presents itself to many of us.

This discouraging and unattractive scenario under-standably alienates many people from any engagement with religion and, quite mistakenly, with spirituality also. From the mystics, we learn that the idea we normally associate with religion is primarily a question of discover-ing who we are. The uncomfortable duality of doing one thing but thinking that we should be doing another can then disappear. Peace and joy are available to us in their deepest and most abiding form for the first time. This is the meaning of the words, 'the truth will set you free' (John: 8.32) in the Gospels. Far from being an obstacle to our true enjoyment of life, spirituality is suddenly perceived as its ultimate and unique source. Every spiritual tradition since the dawn of time has proclaimed this fact. If this fundamental misconception were to be corrected, the quality of life on earth would be altered beyond anything we can possibly imagine at present. In the search for happiness, the limitless quest for the 'outer' would be replaced by an equally determined search for the 'inner'. Simplicity in all its forms would be the natural and inevitable outcome. An altogether different measure of 'standard of living' would emerge reflecting a modified notion of what constitutes 'quality'.

Ridiculous as this may sound to many people, it is not without precedent. In his wisdom, the king of Bhutan replaced GNP as a measure of progress in the nation by a gross national happiness index far more inclusive of spiritual values. In his view, there could be no accurate assessment of collective well being without this. He made it national policy to maintain a balance between material and spiritual progress. Knowing that such an approach to life would alter the nature of every macro and micro socio-economic challenge we are faced with today, is it impossible to conceive that this could be done elsewhere? The material reality of life would, of course, remain unchanged. *It is what each one of us would expect from it that would be modified.* Why accumulate more, the thinking would go, when you can be more contented with less. Is this remotely possible?

IX

Atheists and non-believers in general will tell you that all this is fanciful nonsense. According to Oxford University evolutionary biologist, Richard Dawkins, we have all evolved from amoeba by a process of the natural selection of 'selfish genes' programmed for survival. The world we live in is the natural outcome of this selfish evolutionary dynamic. Given how things have turned out, this view is highly persuasive. In believing this, however, you are also obliged to accept that the exclusively scientific criterion of the evolutionists is the last word on the nature of reality. One supposes that Albert Einstein, who late in life discovered that certain Buddhist findings dating back thousands of years were similar to his own, would not be willing to do this. In fact, he once said:

> Try and penetrate with our limited means the secrets of nature and you will find that, behind all the discernable laws and connections, there remains something subtle, intangible and inexplicable. Veneration for this force beyond anything we can comprehend is my religion . **I maintain that the cosmic religious feeling is the strongest and noblest motive for scientific research.**[8]

Dawkins is an eloquent defender of the scientific view, but it takes a brave man to believe that he is right and that Lao Tzu, Buddha, Aristotle, Plato, Jesus,

St Augustine, Shakespeare, Leonardo da Vinci, St John of the Cross, Tolstoy, Gandhi, Dante, Goethe, Wordsworth, Huxley, C. G. Jung, T. S. Eliot and the Dalai Lama *have all got it wrong*! E. F. Schumacher, himself an economist, had very strong views on this subject and wrote:

> Evolutionism is not science; it is science fiction, even a kind of hoax. It is a hoax that has succeeded too well and has imprisoned modern man in what looks like an irreconcilable conflict between 'science' and 'religion'. It has destroyed all faiths that pull mankind up and has substituted a faith that pulls mankind down…The inability of modern thought to rid itself of this imposture is a failure which may well cause the collapse of Western civilisation. **For it is impossible for any civilisation to survive without a faith in meanings and values transcending the utilitarianism of material comfort.**[9]

In spite of a scientific establishment that remains confidant that by means of science and technology a 'rosy' future awaits us, the deteriorating quality of life on the planet would seem to point to a far less promising outcome. In small, imperceptible ways, the traditional values of the world have been reversed. We admire ambition and call it 'drive', socially acceptable 'self-interest' camouflages greed and selfishness, pride has become a respectable sense of achievement, modesty is seen as a form of weakness, honesty is working within the law, the arrogant and outspoken are viewed as the strong and self-possessed, being 'smart' is a compliment and so on. Every biblical virtue is disregarded or considered 'unrealistic'.

Thomas Merton, the well-known Christian monk and writer, once described his father, in this way: 'if the values of the world had been the right ones my father would have been some kind of a king'. This was not only a moving tribute by a son to a father, but an important statement on how we have turned everything upside down. In a world where egoism and ambition thrive, Merton's father, a good man but a struggling artist, was unable to find his place in society. This inversion of values and the disappearance of an inner sense of 'self' has reduced more and more people to the frantic quest to appear 'successful' by means of outward symbols of wealth, sophistication and refinement. The current obsession with brand names, designer labels, and cosmetic surgery has been the inevitable outcome. The advertising industry, always on the lookout for the weak link in human nature, thrives on this kind of susceptibility. It's a psychological certainty that the growing devotion of time, energy and money to such things and the explosion of the luxury goods industry in recent times, correlates ominously with a disappearing inner identity and a resulting sense of personal emptiness on an unprecedented scale. It would seem that the 'appearance' of something is now considered a legitimate substitute for its substance. The truly negative aspect of this inner void is the fact that it gives rise to pride. Of all human failings it is the single greatest barrier to personal fulfilment and happiness that exists. Envy and jealousy, its twin derivatives, have caused havoc in human relations throughout history and still do. It comes as no surprise to find that Shakespeare, a psychologist without equal in literature, constantly chose to explore the different manifestations of these all-too-human traits in his plays. But to have pride is not our fate. It is the result of a fundamental 'faithlessness', arising from identification with the ego and an exclusively material vision of reality. The constant scramble for 'earthly' distinctions, the principal action of pride, exists only to compensate for an absent sense of 'self'. A person who is 'whole' and at one with a dimension of being that is not self-consciously personal and egoistic, does not experience the need to affirm himself in this way. By definition, what we call 'wholeness' does not authentically exist unless it is so natural that the person does not recognise that he or she possess it. St Augustine implied as much when he said, that 'there is in man a deep spirit so profound as to be hidden even to him in whom it is.' There can be no sense of merit or superiority, therefore. According to the Taoists of ancient China, in our natural state, there are no achievements and no accomplishments; there is only appropriate action. Consciousness becomes the expression of Universal Will. There are no ulterior motives. Doing good deeds is as natural as breathing. Chuang Tzu summed it up as follows:

The man in whom Tao acts without impediment harms no other being by his actions yet he does not know himself to be 'kind', to be 'gentle'.[10]

Lacking 'wholeness', behind smokescreens of 'self-confidence', the hollow nature of most people's belief in themselves becomes rapidly apparent. How can it be otherwise? The ephemeral, ever-altering outer material conditions of our lives can't possibly represent who we are in essence. *The only thing we truly possess is our spiritual identity.* When we fail to recognise this we are empty shells and in the depths of our beings we feel it. Incalculable harm in the world is caused by the vain attempt to compensate for this psychological void. Beyond the multiple forms of clinical insanity, this is the most commonplace psychological disorder that exits. It was recently commented on CNBC, the American financial news channel, that the large drop in the value of shares on the U. S. stock market in early 2009 had caused a precipitous drop in self-esteem by investors. What this means is that the inherent qualities of a person are suddenly of no consequence in their own estimation of themselves relative to the changing value of their personal wealth! The value of 'being' has been entirely supplanted by the importance of 'having'. That statement may well have passed unnoticed in the flow of financial news, but it is full of significance, and an astonishing measure of the degree by which we have been diminished by the tidal wave of material values bearing down on us.

X

The abnegation of a true (spiritual) identity tends to gives rise to two main factors. One is the tendency to personalize things in the very opposite way from that of the Taoists. Being a respected and admired 'someone' in the eyes of others, is somehow felt to compensate for the unappealing prospect of being 'no one' in a world that only recognises the fruits of the ego. For example, the rich are more often willing to separate themselves from their money provided their names are attached to a hospital, library or a university. At a certain level of charity, anonymous donors are a rare species. Charity abounds in wealthy nations but when it concerns large sums of money, it is invariably a calculated affair. There are many and varied motives for being charitable, but rarely is pure compassion one of them. When was the last time a major donor, wishing to raise the standard of living of others, accepted to lower his own? For the same reason, the biblical suggestion that when asked for your coat, you give your shirt also, finds no resonance in our societies.

Organised charity in the West is what it is. It is far better that money changes hands to the benefit of the needy for the wrong reasons than not at all. My point here, is that what might seem an exception to the rule of human egoism is not so in the least. Charity is an instrument of the ego in affluent societies, and, perhaps, more powerfully so by virtue of the fact that it comes in the guise of goodness and generosity. One mustn't forget that while the ego prevails, 'image' counts for everything in the conduct of human affairs. There is nothing more beneficial for a personal or corporate image than to be perceived as charitable or as willing to support worthy causes. Sizeable donations and sponsorships are often a small price to pay to obscure greed and abuse on a far larger scale. In the end, public relations initiatives of this order come down to sound business practice.

The other notable tendency of the ego is the need to assert our presence in the world by arousing the adulation and envy of others. The quest for fame and celebrity has become, therefore, the unchallenged obsession of our time. Lucrative industries such as people magazines, intrusive photography, star academies and reality shows have sprouted everywhere to cater for this. An inner spiritual void now drives millions of people throughout the world to live vicariously through the joys, trials and tribulations of their admired celebrities. Twitter, a recent communication network on the Internet used by many stars, allows fans to have near-continuous access to their lives and thoughts. Different kinds of reality shows now offer the possibility of short moments of notoriety to virtually anyone. In fact, people can now make a living from drawing attention to themselves in the most bizarre and shocking situations.

In a recent *Time* article, John Poniewozik wrote: 'Modern media did not invent lust for attention…Only in the realty-TV era has unstable behaviour become a career choice.' Our spiritual poverty has reached such epic proportions, it seems, that people are willing to tolerate any number of indignities to achieve this. It's not uncommon to find someone who is proud to be considered a 'bimbo,' (which translates to 'imbecile'), or even a porn star, provided the cameras are flashing or they see their name on a billboard. The desperate quest for celebrity has even spawned the phenomenon of being famous for being famous, the prize accorded to those who look the part and are always in the right place at the right time. This has become an ambition for many. Only an inner void of startling proportions can account for a pathological search for affirmation of this nature. It is doomed from the start, however. The ego holds out great promise but there is never an ultimate reward. As Eckhart Tolle points out:

> Nothing can satisfy the ego for long. As long as it runs your life, there are two ways of being unhappy. Not getting what you want is one. Getting what you want is the other."[11]

A special mention must being given to art (and artists) in the modern world. Here again, the ego plays a very prominent role. The personal 'vision' of the artist, in fact his or her whole personal 'story', is now of major importance in determining the 'significance' of his work. Artistic 'expression' has become an orgy of narcissism and gathered immense respect for itself in the process. Pablo Picasso, one of the undisputed masters of the 20th century, was a hugely egotistic and self-centred individual. Fame during his lifetime stoked his desire for riches and he tirelessly produced a huge body of work in his long life, every piece of which is treated like a treasure today. He was not, however, duped by the adulation accorded to him. In a moment of surprising lucidity, he wrote a letter to Giovanni Papini, an Italian journalist, denouncing his own art, confessing that he was merely using his innate virtuosity to exploit the susceptibility of his contemporaries. In his own words:

> In art the public is no longer looking for consolation and exaltation; but the refined, the rich, the idler, the distillers of quintessence look for the new, the strange, the original, the extravagant, the scandalous. And myself, since cubism and after, I satisfied these masters and these critics, with all kinds of extravagant whims that passed through my head; and the less they understood the more I was admired. By means of amusing myself with all these games, with all this nonsense, with all these puzzles, riddles and arabesques, I became famous and quite rapidly. Fame for the painter signifies sales, profit, fortune, riches. And today, as you know, I am famous and rich. But

when I am alone with myself, I do not have the courage to consider myself an artist. I am only a public entertainer who has understood his times and exploited as best he could the imbecility, the vanity, the cupidity, of his contemporaries.[12]

Vincent Van Gogh, on the other hand, lived in a small, bare room in Arles and never sold a painting in his life. If it wasn't for his brother who supported him financially, he could never have pursued his art at all. Nowadays, a bidet hanging in a museum or two strokes of painting on a piece of canvas (or none at all) will fill pages of art magazines with convoluted and incomprehensible praise for the 'vision' and genius of the artist. It can also sell for millions of dollars. In the mad rush to be original, everything from the spurious to the obscene falls within the definition of 'art'. If there is one area of human affairs that has lost its way to an unfathomable degree, it is surely the world of art. In the quest to enjoy 'culture', millions flock to galleries and museums on a daily basis to bear witness, in varying states of shock and bewilderment, to the bizarre, incomprehensible and, at times, offensive examples of modern art. Picasso himself did not seem to have a high opinion of these offerings when he said, 'museums are just a lot of lies, and the people who make art their business are mostly imposters.' Very few people, however, have the courage and conviction to denounce the emperor for not wearing clothes.

For centuries, artistic creation, though not anonymous,

as in the middle-ages, subscribed to a long tradition of artistic values and did not hinge on the personality of the artist. From pre-historic cave paintings to the Impressionists, light, volume and colour, the essential elements of 'form' were derived from Nature. Cezanne once commented,

> Nature as it is seen, nature as it is felt, has to fuse in order to endure, in order to live that life, half human, half divine which is the life of art or if you will, the life of God...The painter owes allegiance to that alone. **Never the logic of the brain. If he abandons himself to that logic, he's lost.** [13]

The idea that art could be 'intellectual', that it could be the expression of the self-indulgent fantasies of the artist would have been anathema. Notwithstanding, modern art is founded on this form of artistic freedom.

Paul Cezanne, the greatest and perhaps one of the last of the upholders of the great tradition of art, clearly expressed the belief that should he allow his personal feelings, thoughts and ideas to intervene when he was painting, his creativity would be impaired. Joachim Gasquet, in a conversation with the artist, recalled the following comments by Cezanne:

> Painting must give us the flavour of Nature's eternity. So I join together nature's straying hands. I select colours, tones and shades. I set them down. I bring them together. They make lines. They become objects without my thinking about them. If I feel the least

distraction, the least weakness, above all, if I interpret too much one day, if today I am carried away by a theory, that is contrary to the day before, **if I think while painting, if I intervene, why then everything is gone.**[14]

The clear implication here was that the ego has no place in the creative process. The quality of transcendence present in all great works of art arises from this fact and is intrinsic to art itself. Art is not art without it. There should be nothing surprising about this, however. The wisdom teachings have uniformly proclaimed this to be true about the process of living. Art merely embodies and expresses the same truth. The present day art establishment, however, has never deviated from its wholehearted dedication to the opposite belief, offering us such 'artistic' wonders as sheep in formaldehyde, framed excrement and other degrading examples of the 'personal' vision' of contemporary artists. If ever we were looking for a tell-tale sign that human decadence and folly had peaked and the demise of our civilisation was not far off, this would be it.

XI

As we have seen, the ego, as an illusory substitute for 'being', is incapable of animating our souls or giving us a glimpse of the potential of life beyond the prosaic and one-dimensional reality we mostly inhabit. In the early part of the last century, Eugen Herrigel, a German Professor of Philosophy lived several years in Japan studying Zen Buddhism and archery with the legendary Master Anzawa. What he learned after a long period of initiation was that in archery, as in life, he wouldn't be able to 'hit the target', (achieve spiritual integrity) without allowing the target and himself to become one. This could only happen by ceasing to desire the perfect shot (relinquishing the ego), so that letting go of the arrow became a natural and effortless gesture of 'being'. He described his initiation into the esoteric world of Zen, almost unheard of in the West at that time, in a very fine little book called *Zen in the Art of Archery*, a classic in its genre.

There is a vital message in what he wrote. One is brought to the understanding that whatever we undertake in the spirit of Zen, be it a high or a lowly task, will bring its full measure of fulfilment, not on account of the action itself, but by virtue of it *being a pure expression of the non-egoic self*. Zen masters, when asked to describe the nature of enlightenment, will typically answer, 'when you eat, you eat, when you walk, you walk.' Behind such an obscure and puzzling response lies the essence of Zen wisdom. Being in the moment, whether we are raking leaves or running corporations, is the portal to higher states of consciousness (God). Allowing our subjective personal agenda — likes, dislikes, ambitions, regrets and so on, to interrupt the natural unfolding reality of existence is to inhibit 'being'. D. T. Suzuki, who was one of the first teachers of Zen Buddhism in the West, described this reality as follows:

> Man is a thinking reed but his great works are done when he is not calculating and thinking. 'Childlikeness' has to be restored after long years of training in the art of self-forgetfulness. When this is attained man **thinks yet he does not think**.[15]

In much the same way, when Zen teacher Shunryu Suzuki wrote: 'In the beginner's mind there are many possibilities, in the experts mind there are few',[16] he, too, was suggesting that the essence of spirituality is Tao-like and spontaneous 'openness'. The expert, by resorting to the mind and being self-consciously 'clever', removes himself from that magical dimension of being. His possibilities then are limited.

All the same, our tenure on earth obliges us to accept certain material responsibilities and carry out obligations to family and society. By Zen standards, on account of a mistaken sense of self through identification with the ego, all this has been carried out in an imperfect manner. What convention doesn't recognise, however, is that those obligations in themselves have never been the principal objectives of life nor what gives it meaning. This is why a materially comfortable life can, at times, seem so 'flat'. No matter to what extent people keep themselves 'busy', a certain *ennui* tends to seep into their lives causing problems such as alcoholism, violence, depression, extra-marital affairs and so on. It is almost certain that this is the underlying cause of an epidemic of infidelity and the high rates of divorce in our western societies, no matter what other reasons are cited. It is an inescapable fact that fulfilment in the deepest sense can only come from a life lived as an expression of the self defined by Professor Herrigel, Suzuki and the Taoists. Such 'being' is like the electricity that lights up a lamp or the sunlight that permits plants to grow and become food. By living in and through our egos, we become lamps that give no light and plants that provide no nourishment — to ourselves in the first place. We are intelligent machines, the kind that can accomplish surgical wonders and go to the moon but we still don't know how to live. One hundred and sixty years of extraordinary industrial and technological growth has both liberated and enslaved us to a degree we seem unable to recognise or measure. Professor Herrigel describes the predicament of mankind in the following passage:

It began by his disregarding or misunderstanding the deepest purpose of existence. No other creature is constituted by nature, as he is, not only to live spontaneously from the centre of being, but in spontaneous understanding of the whole of life, to reveal the secret of all existence. He has been granted the ultimate possibility of bursting the bonds of his individuality, of entering into intimate contact with everything that is, of encountering everywhere in the external world something akin to him, of perceiving himself in this kinship and becoming aware of this centre of being, so that **he lives as much as he is lived**.[17]

Some years ago, commenting on his novel, *More Die of Heartbreak*, at an interview, Saul Bellow said that one of the subjects of the book was 'the difference between a fabricated person and a true person'. He then took his cue from Nietzsche who said that in traditional societies people were governed by some kind of overriding faith in the spiritual order of things but that in modern societies, released from all such allegiances, people were 'free to make themselves up'. This mirage with all its negative consequences is the so-called freedom we enjoy in the West. Freedom is only liberation when it is the freedom to live out a meaningful state of being that has roots in a Universal Order. Referring to this fundamental spiritual principle, Goethe stated, 'Law alone can make you free'.

Where this is not the case, (and a belief in social ideals such as democracy, justice, capitalism, prosperity for all and so on, is not what I am referring to), freedom becomes a handicap. We don't, in effect, know what to do with it. The sports industry, Las Vegas and the entertainment business in general are the great beneficiaries of this predicament. The point is that we are not naturally constituted to live in a vacuum of faith or real purpose, unengaged in the meaningful labours of existence outside the context of family and community. The emancipating benefits of economic and technological development have gone too far in separating us from this natural process of living. We are then left in an empty and disoriented inner state that gives rise to the disorders referred to earlier. Of these, 'suggestibility' in its varying forms is the most direct consequence of this inner disarray. It is also the most widespread and harmful in its effects and by no means the province of the simple-minded or uneducated. Far from it, in fact.

Adherence to strange sects is an extreme example of the dangers of suggestibility, but it deserves a mention when you discover that doctors, lawyers and PhD's are found to be members of sects that believe in such things as dialogue with visitors from outer space, vacations in flying saucers and so on. Less exotic, but just as surprising, you find that organisations such as Scientology have a considerable following among otherwise educated, intelligent and sophisticated people. On a more mundane level, suggestibility is at its most dangerous when media manipulation leaves an enormous number of people unable to distinguish the true from the false in the world of politics. Dr. Maurice Nicoll, one of the early believers in psychological medicine, wrote:

> When there is no inner life one passes into the power of outer life completely. Man becomes helpless — a creature of mass-movements, mass-politics, of gigantic mass-organisations.[18]

And it's happening all the time. George W. Bush would never have been re-elected to a second term in office in the Unites States if the Republican party hadn't mounted the most extensive programme of slander, mis-information and fear-mongering that the world has ever seen. Only suggestibility on a vast scale allows such things to happen. Fascism in one form or another will always raise its ugly head while suggestibility continues to be an unavoidable consequence of the way we think and live.

As form and substance are often hard to reconcile in the public arena, the U S presidential elections have become long, complex and expensive operations. The 'image' of a candidate is of paramount importance and becomes the decisive factor in a successful campaign. When appearance fails to correspond with reality, millions of dollars are mobilised to bridge the gap. A slip-up here or a misinterpreted statement there, can threaten a candidate's chances in an instant, calling for more millions of dollars in media coverage to repair the damage. The electorate becomes putty in a child's hand. Highly effective but often unscrupulous campaign managers and advisors are able to make people believe that day is night, as was the case with Bush. The question of credibility in politics ends up being more to do with making a candidate consistent with his projected image than vice versa.

Election politics has become something of a charade, therefore, providing us with leaders who do little more than mirror our general confusion as to means and ends. They are rarely able to do anything but perpetuate the status quo. Nancy Gibbs of *Time* magazine describes Washington as 'a capital whose day-to-day functioning has become part-travesty, part tragedy, wasteful, blind, vain, petty'. Rare then are the politicians who can raise our expectations and inspire us by acting from deeply held convictions that go against the tide of history. There have been some notable examples, of course. Men such as Abraham Lincoln, Martin Luther King, Mahatma Gandhi and Nelson Mandela, far from reflecting the collective failings of their societies, have been an inspiration to men and women throughout the world. Unlike many, they possessed the spiritual stature to elevate us beyond our habitual selfishness, prejudice and shortsightedness. 'Nothing is more powerful than an individual acting out of his conscience, thus helping to bring the collective conscience to life,' said political journalist Norman Cousins. By changing hearts as well as minds such men were able to change the course of history. In these challenging times, who would not wish that Barack Obama will prove to be one of them?

XII

In the 1950's and 60's 'alienation' was a popular concept among sociologists. It seemed to announce the spiritual dislocation we are witnessing today. With rapid post-war industrialisation and the advent of technology, life in urban society was drained of much that nourishes the soul in the name of a new and more affluent way of living. The term 'alienation' is used more rarely nowadays but the condition it described not only persists, but has also developed with increasingly harmful consequences. The untidy, irrational human needs such as ancient beliefs, reverence and communion with nature, as well as traditions and folklore resulting from both, were considered impediments to progress. They were made to disappear by the false promise of the *'freedom to re-invent ourselves'*, as if it were possible to suddenly devise a blueprint for living and calculate human needs like a mathematical formula. In the pursuit of this mirage, 'lifestyles' and careers unrelated to any traditional occupation of family or community were arbitrarily adopted, breaking with centuries-old habits and rituals of living.

The subsequent emergence of standardized, rootless and spiritually disconnected communities, urban and suburban, has had a devastating effect on the psychic health of society. In modern society, beyond a superficial cordiality, there is very little interaction between people who live in physical proximity of each other. All semblance of emotional interdependence, the only basis for a truly human exchange between people living in community, has vanished. Neighbours become strangers to one another, islands of physical and psychological isolation and indifference. As these developments served the needs of commerce and a growing prosperity, the fundamental changes in living habits were not questioned. One of the most harmful consequences of this newly conditioned social character was the disintegration of 'love' in our culture. In its authentic form, love has become a relatively rare phenomenon nowadays. Relationships founded on sentimentality, 'passion' or self-interest are far more common. Marriage is often viewed in a practical sense as 'teamwork', what psychologist Erich Fromm describes as an 'exchange of personality packages in the hope of a fair bargain'. In spite of ever higher rates of divorce, such relationships can and do endure at times but often in a loveless manner. People are divorced in their hearts long before they physically separate. Nevertheless, the capacity to love remains an essential necessity of mankind.

Traditional societies in the emerging countries are often far more apprehensive at the idea that they could go down the same path, than we tend to believe. These societies are caught in the difficult dilemma of wanting to improve the material conditions of life while maintaining their traditions. This makes them vulnerable to the deadening logic of pure commerce and business that along with its goods and services exports its empty, materialistic ideology with little concern for such sensitivities. India's initial refusal to have Wal-Mart implant itself there is a small but meaningful example. The spread of Wal-Mart would sound the death knell of individually creative, local and artisanal economies throughout the third world. These would be replaced by cheap, standardized goods, destroying a whole way of life rich in traditions and folklore that maintains the social equilibrium of entire communities. Why should the way of western commerce, so harmful to our own spiritual condition, be considered desirable in parts of the world where this is not yet the case? Rather than alleviating poverty, such measures serve only to accentuate its effects by altering the nature of the human context that exists. All human activity, even the exchange of goods and services between people, must answer to the requirements of the soul. In the western industrial and technological cultures, we have neglected this simple truth at some cost to the quality of our lives. We remain, however, quite oblivious to this fact as columnist William Pfaff writes:

> It is inconceivable to the liberals and the conservatives of modern society that the traditional world, in which everyone except themselves lives, remains a valid choice for those who live in it…Americans believe that economic success automatically promotes

human success. Trade is believed overwhelmingly benevolent in part because America's leadership can scarcely imagine a valid alternative to the materialism and political values of the modern West.

In this state of myopia and by measuring 'progress' in material terms alone, we don't seem to be able to recognise the spiritual dearth within our own societies. 'The tragedy of life is what dies inside a man while he lives,' observed Einstein. In fact, our so-called 'high' standard of living should be viewed more accurately as a high standard of death (of the soul). What has taken place in modern society, I can't describe more eloquently, or with more wry humour, than the following paragraphs by Wendell Berry in his book *The Unsettling of America*. Written more than thirty years ago, this depiction of a 'fortunate' average citizen of the modern world is as relevant as ever:

> The disease of the modern character is specialization. The first, and best known, hazard of the specialist system is that it produces specialists — people who are elaborately and expensively trained to do one thing. We get into absurdity very quickly here. There are, for instance, educators who have nothing to teach, communicators who have nothing to say, medical doctors skilled at expensive cures for diseases that they have no skill, and no interest, in preventing. More common, and more damaging, are the

inventors, manufacturers, and salesmen of devices who have no concern for the possible effects of those devices. Specialization is thus seen to be a way of institutionalising, justifying and paying highly for a calamitous disintegration and scattering — out of the various functions of character: workmanship, care, conscience and responsibility.

Even worse, a system of specialization requires the abdication to specialists of various competences and responsibilities that were once personal and universal. Thus, the average — one is tempted to say, the ideal — American citizen now consigns the problem of food production to agribusiness men, the problems of health to doctors and sanitation experts, the problems of education to school teachers and educators, and so on. This supposedly fortunate citizen is therefore left with only two concerns: making money and entertaining himself. He earns money, typically, working an eight-hour day at a job for the quality or consequences of which somebody else — or, perhaps, more typically, nobody else — will be responsible. And not surprisingly, since he can do so little else for himself, he is even unable to entertain himself, for there exists an enormous industry of exorbitantly expensive specialists whose purpose is to entertain him.

The fact is, however, that this is probably the most unhappy average citizen in the history of

the world. He has not the power to provide himself with anything but money. From morning to night he does not touch anything he has produced himself, in which he can take pride. For all his leisure and recreation, he feels bad, he looks bad, he is over-weight, and his health is poor. His air, water and food are all known to contain poisons. He suspects that his love life is not as fulfilling as other people's. He wishes he had been born sooner, or later. He does not know why his children are the way they are. He does not understand what they say. He does not care much and does not know why he does not care. He does not know what his wife wants or what he wants. Certain advertisements and pictures in magazines make him suspect that he is basically unattractive. He does not know what he would do if he lost his job, if the economy failed, if the utility companies failed, if the police went on strike, if his wife left him…And for these anxieties, of course, he consults certified experts, who in turn consult certified experts about their *anxieties*. **It is rarely considered that this average citizen is anxious because he ought to be…!**"[19]

As with all caricatures, Wendell Berry's description is devastatingly close to the truth. This dispiriting picture, shared to one degree or another by all industrial societies, would seem to be the dubious 'reward' for becoming the wealthiest nations on earth and by believing that we can organise life without proper regard for the human spirit.

As desirable as it may seem in principle, the difficulty is that we cannot impose 'simplicity' on ourselves by a simple act of will. It won't work. An authentic life, of which simplicity is one important aspect, must evolve naturally from within. Willpower is a formidable instrument of achievement in the material world, but in matters concerning the spirit, only a shift in consciousness can bring this about. The inertia created by centuries of identification with ego weighs heavily on humanity, making it is almost impossible for this to occur spontaneously. The dysfunctions within the social system that are now coming to a head, the near collapse of the financial system in 2008 being only a recent example, must in time force a change of direction upon us. That moment of truth approaches. If our grandchildren are to survive on this planet, we must experiment, not with a new way of thinking but with *a new way of being*. In that sense, the problems we face today present us with a rare opportunity to make fundamental changes. It's interesting to note in this regard that the Chinese expression for crisis consists of the symbol for *danger* and the symbol for *opportunity*. Mahatma Gandhi was reported to have said, 'We must BE the change we want to see in the world'. Nothing sums up the situation better than these few words. At this point, there's not a plan, programme or policy issuing from governments that can make this happen. The requirements of mankind have shifted to a higher plane.

The responsibility now lies with each individual.

In fact, it is the very nature of consciousness that must be examined. The mystics have repeatedly told us that in our 'normal' state of consciousness, we are not 'awake'. Clearly, for most people, this is a startling assertion. At one level, it's incomprehensible. After all, who can deny that we behave expediently and, for the most part, rationally, in our normal state of consciousness? What the mystics are telling us, however, is something that conventional psychology doesn't acknowledge. To be awake in spiritual terms means *becoming conscious of being conscious*. In essence, this means that a state of 'awareness' must co-exist with normal states of consciousness. We are then able to generate a very high quality of energy that elevates consciousness to a different level of being. Without 'awareness', this is not possible. It is not a matter of being concentrated or alert. T. S. Eliot understood this when he wrote, 'to be conscious is not to be in time'.(Burnt Norton 11).

By allowing a space to exist between 'awareness' and consciousness, we interrupt the continuous process of identification of our thoughts and feelings with everything we do. The action of the ego rooted in 'unconsciousness' (conventional consciousness) is then momentarily suspended. 'Awakened' consciousness, what the mystics refer to as 'being', operates with a far greater sensitivity. This enhanced awareness enables us to sense who we are in an entirely different way. The individualised 'self' melts into a greater, all-encompassing whole *where all is perceived as one.* The sensation of joy that accompanies this experience is altogether different from what we normally experience in moments of elation. It is what is referred to in the Bible as 'the peace that passes all understanding' (Philippians: 4 .7) or simply, *'love'*. It is also the nature of Enlightenment, Satori, Nirvana, the Kingdom of Heaven, call it what you will. In fact, this is the object of all non-conventional religious practice. It is what all the founders of the great spiritual traditions were teaching their followers, only to have their message misinterpreted or distorted over the centuries. The insanity of religious conflict, the principle cause of violence in the world, is that the *original* message is essentially the same everywhere and has never changed. *Truth is and has always been One.*

It is hardly believable that we have been at odds with each other for thousands of years over differences in belief that have no objective reason to exist. But the extent of the folly doesn't end there. The institutionalisation of religion has codified and ritualised these errors of interpretation to such a degree, that conventional religion has been rendered sterile and no longer offers genuine spiritual 'uplift'. There is no place for mysticism in conventional religious practice. In spite of this, hundreds of millions of people regularly practice some form of religion throughout the world but rarely, if ever, is there any inner transformation, which is its only true objective. Religion stripped of mysticism is like trying to fly without wings. For example, is it possible to believe that Jesus of

Nazareth, a humble carpenter, would approve of the power, opulence and hierarchy of the Papacy and consider it as being his legitimate representation on earth? The sad truth is that the Church has reduced the living essence of Christ's teaching, its mystical significance, to a turgid and lifeless repetition of prayers and blessings, discouraging to all true spiritual seekers. For this reason hundreds of thousands of people have abandoned traditional religions. That the Catholic Church can still maintain its 'spiritual' authority over billions of people can only be viewed as a glaring testament to the prevailing levels of 'unconsciousness' in the world'.

XIII

It is quite understandable that in normal states of consciousness the notion of 'enlightenment' would seem preposterous. The main reason for this is the abiding belief that our normal conscious condition encompasses all of our cognitive possibilities. In one narrow sense, it does. Spiritual consciousness, as defined earlier, operates on a different level, which is to say, not only in response to our mind but to our feelings and emotions as well, all acting as one. To apprehend things in this way is the essence of mysticism. Centuries of rationalism have left us severely handicapped in this respect. In the West, because of our tendency towards 'cleverness' built on scientific rationalism we have failed to develop certain deep instincts that have existed in some traditional societies in the past. As a result, these instincts, vitally important in sensing the 'wholeness' of life, have had no role to play in the development of the world we know. 'The intuitive mind is a sacred gift and the rational mind is a faithful servant. We have created societies that honour the servant but has forgotten the gift,' said Einstein. The ego-based consciousness, has fashioned not only our present materialistic way of life, but an entire civilisation and always in a manner that fails to reflect the extraordinary potential of men and women 'made in the image of God'.

G. I. Gurdjieff, one of the most influential spiritual teachers of the last century, described the situation as follows:

> A European's understanding of an object observed by him is formed exclusively by means of an all-round 'mathematical informedness' about it, whereas most of the people of certain (traditional) societies grasp the essence of an object sometimes with their feelings and sometimes even solely by instinct. It is a great pity that the present period of culture which we call 'European civilisation', is, in the whole process of the perfecting of humanity, as it were, an empty and abortive interval.[21]

From our first to our last moment on earth, the reality of life presents itself in egoic terms exclusively. Education, as we know it, is the product of this reality and has no purpose other than to prepare us for it. Take, for example, the prevailing belief that more is better. Contemporary conditions of life conspire in making us believe that we are better off if we are richer, more educated, more widely travelled, have more possessions, look better, live longer and so on. In very few instances is it considered that our lives can be improved by having *less* of anything. And yet, in psychologically verifiable terms, this is true. We must move beyond the *idée fixe* that we are inherently greedy, selfish, and proud and that these destructive instincts serve us well.

This simply doesn't conform to the message handed

down to us through the ages by mystics and wise men of all traditions informing us of the opposite. Today it is urgent that we heed their message. Unless we can collectively find greater contentment from possessing less and living more simply in accordance with our true spiritual nature, our very survival on this planet is in question. From where we are at present, this would entail a great spiritual leap for the vast majority of men and women on earth, but without it there is no way out of our current 'impasse'. For the first time in human history, the deteriorating psychological condition of humanity is having a destructive impact not only on the stability of the social and economic structures in place, but on the ecological equilibrium of the planet as well. Eco-systems throughout the world are collapsing. Extreme climate disturbance and unpredictability is now a daily reality. The social and economic consequences of both have been devastating and human suffering is on the increase.

What then are the prospects for humanity? Without change, it's only hopeful to those still clinging to the delusional view that with the help of renewed capital flows, further globalisation, new technology and so on, we will pick up where we left off and continue to squeeze additional wealth from our exhausted planet into the future. This is just not realistic. For the vast majority of people the situation is bad and getting worse by the day. The finite resources of the planet have been depleted. We have scarred and polluted the earth irreversibly. At any one time, there are dozens of armed conflicts going on in the world causing untold misery to millions. In the third world, those not suffering the consequences of war are living in extreme poverty or dying of famine or diseases. Climate change, for which we are all responsible, is going to exacerbate the situation by rendering large swathes of the planet uninhabitable. The minority of people, who are fortunate enough to have 'higher' standards of living, suffers in ever greater numbers from a variety of psychological disorders such as depression or physical ones such as obesity. Furthermore, we divorce each other in ever greater numbers for less and less good reason, suffer loss from the greed of those entrusted with our money, overpay or underpay each other causing intolerable inequalities of wealth, health, and opportunity, and, finally, hate and kill each other on the basis of colour, creed or ethnic origin. These are the consequences of our present state of unconsciousness and the list is by no means exhaustive. Human excellence, exists, of course, but is so rare that it can barely be taken into account in an assessment of this nature. Who can deny that the need for change is urgent?

XIV

Fragile as the economic system of the world proved itself to be in September 2008, and unpredictable and murderous as is terrorism and the wars it has provoked, nothing threatens humanity on the scale and magnitude of climate change. In spite of all the rhetoric, one is obliged to conclude that this fact remains largely unacknowledged at present. Hundreds of billions of dollars were spent to vanquish Saddam Hussein and occupy Iraq. Countless additional billions are being spent conducting a war in Afghanistan. In the meantime, climate irregularity, the precursor of cataclysmic climate change to come, is already causing widespread havoc, death and suffering throughout the world. And yet, the problem is not considered urgent enough to justify a comparable resolve or investment.

Many people remain confused on the issue largely because the scientific establishment is divided on whether human activity is responsible for global warming. A couple of cold winters and you have some people considering the whole matter to be a hoax. For many others it remains an abstraction too far removed from their daily reality to require prompt and determined action. In times of economic recession it further loses priority. This uncertainty is understandable but irrelevant. Climate change is a reality no matter whom or what is causing it.

The real danger is that by abstracting humanity as the cause, we will continue to plunder the planet and inflict further ecological damage with a decreased sense of responsibility.

The fluctuations in temperature in most parts of the western world are not really indicative of what's going on. The real drama of climate change is being played out in the Antarctic Peninsula, Central Asia and Greenland and there it is a different story altogether. According to Dr Gino Casassa, a leading Chilean glaciologist and a member of the Intergovernmental Panel on Climate Change, temperatures in these areas are rising ten times faster than the global average. Grass is starting to grow in Antarctica's barren soil. Glaciers are visibly retreating. In the summer it rains more often than it snows. To give a measure of the threat, the Larsen Ice shelf eighty-seven kilometres long collapsed and disappeared seven years ago in as little as three weeks. Scientists believe that the entire West Antarctic ice sheet, comprising nearly one fifth of the continent, is at risk. If it were to break up, sea levels could rise by six metres. This could happen in as little as ten years or in as much as fifty to eighty years. The point is that sooner or later there is a very high probability that it will happen. The truth is that scientists can't keep up with the accelerating rate of change. In 2004 the International Energy Agency projected that China would exceed the US in CO_2 emissions by 2030. *It did so in 2007!*

For those people sunning themselves at South Beach in Miami, the prospect that a good part of Florida would find itself underwater must seem so remote as to be no real cause for concern today. You would think, however, that even the distant possibility that New York, London, Tokyo and Shanghai could also disappear would constitute a threat of very serious proportions to the international community. Many people set their hopes on the Copenhagen (COP15) Conference in late 2009 as the last chance to establish a serious, binding agenda adhered to by all participants. They were deeply disappointed, however. Jeremy Hobbs, executive director of Oxfam International, summed it up as follows:

> The deal is a triumph of spin over substance. It recognises the need to keep warming below two degrees but does not commit to do so. It pushes back the big decisions on emission cuts and fudges the issue of climate cash (for developing nations).

Clearly, without a widespread sense of urgency from people willing to change their lives in the rich industrialised nations, the political will to do what is necessary will also be absent. Even the effectiveness of measures such as cap and trade, the only arrow at present in the bow of the international community, is questioned. Dr James Hansen, head of the NASA Goddard Institute for Space Research, is vehemently opposed to the Carbon Market schemes negotiated in Copenhagen. 'Because cap and trade is enforced through the selling and trading of permits, it actually perpetuates the pollution it is supposed to eliminate', he says. Furthermore, he is highly critical of politicians who won't acknowledge the full measure of the problem and treat it as anything less than the moral challenge of the 21st century. He goes on to say:

> We don't have a leader who is able to grasp it and say what is really needed. Instead they are trying to continue business as usual. This is analogous to the issue of slavery faced by Abraham Lincoln or the issue of Nazism faced by Winston Churchill. On those kinds of issues you cannot compromise. You can't say let's reduce slavery, let's find a compromise and reduce it by forty or fifty per cent.

The real cause of this myopia lies at the heart of the problem itself. Man-made global warming from CO_2 emissions is so closely linked to our personal and collective habits of unlimited consumption and waste that we are unable to conceive of any other way of living. We tinker away on the edges of the problem so as to avoid the inescapable recognition that our growth-based economic system, reliant on the egoism of each one of us, is ultimately doomed. This is a scientific fact not an ideological belief. As Anatol Lieven, senior research fellow at the New America Foundation in Washington put it:

> The entire democratic capitalist system will be seen to have failed utterly as a model for humanity and as a custodian of essential human interests. Underlying

western free-market democracy, and its American form in particular, is the belief that this system is of permanent value to mankind…It is not supposed to serve only the short-term and selfish interests of existing Western populations. If our system is indeed no more than that, then it will pass from history even more completely than Confucian China — and will deserve to do so.

So are we 'fiddling while Rome burns'? There's no doubt. With this civilisation-threatening danger bearing down on us, it's hardly believable that we are still building huge mansions, designing luxury cars and boats, planning to double the airline capacity of the world, lighting up Las Vegas like it's Disneyland and so on. What then should we do? When it finally becomes clear that technological 'fixes' designed to preserve the status quo won't work, we will have reached the limits of the capacity of man's ingenuity to safeguard our civilisation. Once this humbling fact is clearly acknowledged, and it will no doubt take a long succession of catastrophes in the West for this to happen, it will be a crucial turning point for humanity. *We shall then be left with what we have always had and can never be taken away from us — our spiritual nature*. At that point, the only real means we will have at our disposal to confront what lies ahead is to embrace this fact. This may seem a puny measure, from a materialistic point of view. However, a move towards personal and collective simplicity, the very expression of our spiritual nature, would be an extraordinarily powerful development. In light of what would be called for under the circumstances, nothing of a material or technological nature could match its effectiveness. It is, therefore, an urgent necessity.

For the first time in human history, the political solutions of the future must be conditioned exclusively by this reality. What does this mean in practical terms, (I can hear the sceptics say). The answer is — there is no way of knowing in advance. All that can be said with certainty is that to discover an authentic simplicity is to be integrated in a spiritual reality whose nature is perfection. To abide in this reality is to embody the right way to be and act at any moment. What is lost would be nothing. What we would gain would be everything.

XV

Without our being aware of it, the stranglehold of the ego operates through the twin evils of 'attachment' and 'identification'. Through them, we instinctively bind ourselves by thought and emotion to everything that is going on around us and become unaware of ourselves in the process. It is this mechanism that draws us into the drama of life, giving every aspect of it an importance it doesn't deserve. This is the nature of unconsciousness. Life unfolds as a succession of largely inconsequential events determined by such things as a colour we like, a person we dislike, a trip we want to take, the comment we didn't care for, the weather tomorrow, the need to make money, to look younger, to live longer, and so on *ad infinitum*. The needs and desires that control our lives absorbing all our energy and attention arise from the ***wrongly perceived importance of things***. In this way, an entire edifice of self-centred preoccupations develops, shackling us heart, mind and body to the outside world. A contemporary sage, when asked once to explain the key to his wisdom, to the bewilderment of those expecting a profound explanation, answered very simply, 'I don't care what happens'. Detachment from the events happening in one's life is a far greater achievement than this simple response would indicate. The inner 'space' this sage

100

possessed, where all true freedom and psychological independence exist, is the foundation of enlightenment.

Unlike our sage, however, the subjective world most people experience finds itself inextricably entangled with every imaginable form of thought and belief. Fear of the morrow is with us permanently. The web of attachment and identification that we spin robs us of all psychological autonomy. When our essential individuality, our real self, is lost in this way, we respond to life within far narrower parameters of choice and free will than we can understand. Furthermore, we respond in a similar manner to the same stimuli. Whether it is in our opinions, ways of living, habits of consumption, or response to the media, one of the principle characteristics of the egoic world is the tendency to react to everything in standardised ways. This once prompted Oscar Wilde to declare that, 'Most people are other people. Their thoughts are someone else's opinions, their lives a mimicry' (De Profundis). In fact, the uniformity of conventional consciousness is both the cause and the victim of the soulless nature of the way we live.

Over the course of history the world has been fashioned by a blind and relentless expansion of egoistic power, first by conquests, then by commerce and colonisation and finally by industrialisation and the technological revolution. The essential dynamic has never really varied and the beauty and magic of life has been consistently obscured from us in this way. Where once men possessed a profound communion with nature, the ego, in the form of our ruthless predecessors, believing themselves to be civilizers, managed to destroy all connection with this sacred source of life. In *The Course of Empire* Bernard de Voto wrote:

> The first belt-knife given by a European to an Indian was a portent as great as the cloud that mushroomed over Hiroshima…In an instant the man of 6000 BC was bound fast to a way of life that had developed seven and a half millennia beyond his own. **He began to live better and he began to die.**[21]

We, of course, are both the perpetrators and the victims of this act of ignorance, a long drawn out spiritual suicide that will reach its culminating stage perhaps sooner than one thinks. The point is that we are 'dead souls' long before our physical demise. The ego, as we have seen, is an imposter filling the vacuum left by ignorance about who we are. Because of its essentially illusory nature, the moment we recognise this imposture, it vanishes. We then relate to everything in an entirely different way. The difficulty is this will not occur because someone makes the conscious decision to become less egoistic or a 'better' person. There are no twelve-step programmes that will take us there. It happens only when we experience the truth of what the mystics have been telling us for centuries. This form of grace, we are informed, is the reward for a certain kind of openness, simplicity and sincerity. Although there is then an immediate and irreversible transformation, nothing is actually being added to us by this experience. The 'light' we all carry within us from birth can be obscured but never extinguished. When he spoke of those who were harming him, Jesus said, 'they know not what they do' (Luke: 23. 34). This is acting blindly under the influence of the ego. Where ego is absent we experience our 'enlightened' nature spontaneously, prompting St Augustine to have said, 'Love and do what you will' (7th Sermon: First letter of St John). In Christian terms it's called Grace. The state of 'wholeness' referred to in Taoism and Zen is essentially the same thing. Our actions will be appropriate in all circumstances, as St Augustine pointed out, because they are not ours in a personal, individual and egoistic sense. To experience this extraordinary state of being is our birthright. By falling prey to the lure of the ego, we deprive ourselves of this benediction every instant of our lives. 'Miracles are not contrary to nature but only contrary to what we know about nature,' said St Augustine. For what other reason is it written that we are 'made in the image of God' (in Christianity), that 'the Buddha exists in all men' (in Buddhism), that 'you are that', (Tat Vam Asi in Hinduism) as in all the great spiritual traditions? It is long overdue that we inherit the extraordinary reality of who we are. Albert Einstein said, 'there are two ways to live. One is as though nothing is a miracle. The other is as though everything is a miracle'. We have always chosen to believe the former. Isn't it time now to switch? How much more hopeful and rewarding can a prospect be?

Whether we are aware of it or not, however, the Universe is moving inexorably towards this objective. As the laws of cause and effect will not be suspended to accommodate our inability to recognise the situation we have created, the problems we face will only get worse. 'Facts don't cease to exist because they are ignored', said Aldous Huxley. We can go on believing in the illusion of material 'progress' in the old way, and, no doubt, most people will, but as events in the world continue to reveal the negative consequences of this form of consciousness, it will become increasingly difficult to do so. At some point in the near future we shall be obliged to acknowledge that the heedless quest for profit and growth is a destructive mirage and prepare ourselves inwardly for the challenges ahead. It is the only way forward for humanity.

XVI

One of the principal characteristics of an ego–based vision of life is that it takes things very seriously. And well it should, in one sense. Viewed acquisitively and selfishly, life is bound to be uncertain and threatening. Every event in our private lives or in the world at large is interpreted ego-centrically, which is to say, as helping or hindering us. When things go wrong the spectre of failure frightens us. When all is well, fear arises from the anticipation of loss. These sentiments are shared by rich and poor alike, oftentimes more acutely by the rich who have more to lose. This points to the fact that no matter what religion we embrace, the overwhelming evidence suggests that our beliefs fail to generate trust in a spiritual reality. When it comes to determining the course of their lives, most people would still place their faith in the intelligence, talents and will power at their disposal and, perhaps, a dash of luck. Self-reliance, a recognised quality in our capitalist culture, sums it up perfectly.

Church going, a psychological support of importance to many, is largely adapted to accommodate our materialistic and ego-centric ways. The prevailing view, particularly in the United States, is that, provided we obey his wishes, God is there to promote our well being and advance our interests. The *New York Times* columnist David Brooks recently quoted a passage from a 19th Century Baptist minister who delivered a sermon entitled 'Acres of Diamonds' six thousand times to delighted audiences across America, saying:

> I say that you ought to get rich, and it is your duty to get rich…Money is power, and you ought to be reasonably ambitious to have it .You ought, because you can do more good with it than you could without it.

This is what they wanted to hear then, and it's what people want to hear today. So little have things changed in this respect, that one can easily imagine this message being delivered at the present time to thunderous applause in some huge auditorium in Texas. Preachers of varying denominations prosper greatly by exhorting us to take advantage of the benevolence of our material universe. Best sellers offering prescriptions for spiritual and commercial success abound. The potent cocktail of material ambition and 'spirituality' is, of course, well received in a society dedicated to business and commerce. It would even seem to be the perfect formula for addressing the contradictory needs of our conscience and our pockets were it not for the awkward fact that a spiritual reality doesn't work in this way. In the same article in the *New York Times*, David Brooks goes on to inform us that in the middle of the Great Depression Dale Carnegie's book *How to Win Friends and Influence People* sold more copies than any book up to that point other than the Bible. Years later this was followed by *The Power of Positive Thinking* by the Reverend N. V. Peale that was highly recommended as an aid to success. Clearly, pragmatism and faith have somehow become interchangeable. The biblical definition of mammon is money on which a person has placed his or her trust. There is little doubt as to where the faith of the world lies at present.

The Bernard Madoff fraud incident is very instructive in this regard. Although his 'funds' delivered consistent returns that defied rational explanation, the thirst for gain prevailed over caution and good sense even among the most intelligent and, perhaps, the wisest, among us. Nobel Prizewinner, Elie Wiesel, a holocaust survivor, was quoted as saying: 'We gave him everything. We thought he was God'. If through these events we were able to recognise that our appetite for gain brought us to the brink of catastrophe and that we must moderate our expectations, Madoff's Ponzi scheme would have served some purpose. If not, the spiritual hollowness at the core of our society will continue to breed many such cases of pathological dishonesty in the future. 'The centre cannot hold,' W.B. Yeats informed us. Organic shame, a virtue much prized in traditional societies, is long gone. Many people refrain from dishonest activities only from fear of the law. Others, in far greater numbers, acting within the law, have no qualms when it comes to participating in the institutionalization of injustice on a vast scale. The pain caused by the financial crisis of 2008-9 will perhaps make us more aware of the anomalies and injustices that abound in the world, although nothing is less sure.

It is estimated, for example, that the amount of

money Americans spend on cosmetics and pet food alone could feed and educate the rest of the world. Is this sort of thing tolerable in the long run? While we remain anchored to the ego in our present state of consciousness, anomalies of this nature will continue to be acceptable. At the prevailing levels of consciousness there are perfectly reasonable justifications for everything being as it is. Without a spiritual vision of life nothing can ever change. Reason devoid of 'being' has brought us to where we are and it will keep us there. It's now time to become *unreasonable* and think with our hearts not just our minds. 'The salvation of this human world lies nowhere else than in the human heart', said Vaclav Havel. We can't continue to believe, as conventional thinking dictates, that hard work, effort and sacrifice are an adequate justification for accumulating wealth beyond our needs and adding to it at every opportunity. This faithless vision of life is the result of the heart being eclipsed by a mind preoccupied entirely with itself. Rather than having our lives be an expression of the divine universe referred to by the great Taoist and Zen teachers, we miss our calling altogether. 'What does it profit a man to gain the whole world if he loses his soul', said Jesus. Nothing can better define the choices we have in life than this powerful statement from the Gospels. We grasp at certitude in the material world without suspecting that life is a thousand times more magical, unpredictable and beholden to forces far greater than our narrow and sterile vision permits us to understand.

XVII

So it is that a certain absence of joy is common to most people as they go about amusing themselves and having 'fun'. On this question, of course, very few would agree. As everything is built around the false notion that 'success' in life brings happiness, custom and pride dictate the necessity to uphold a positive façade at all times. Such socially conditioned cheerfulness should never be mistaken for genuine serenity, peace or joy, however. It is impossible for the egoic mind to experience these states in an authentic fashion. As it is, we tend to sublimate or conceal our true feelings much of the time. This ambivalence is forced upon us because the ego prevents us from *'accepting'* what befalls us in life. Inner resistance to unfavourable events leads to feelings of frustration, anger and resentment. By creating a space of psychological independence, 'acceptance' alters our relationship to the same objective reality. It was reported that in spite of the unspeakable conditions in the Nazi concentration camps, some victims were said to have experienced states of beatitude. Writer and spiritual teacher, J. G. Bennett explains it as follows:

> The real thing about suffering is that it enables an action to proceed in the depths in us; it enables us to

get below the surface, to find the place where there is no suffering. Not-suffering means to have entered into the sacred place inside us where there is no suffering **because it is a place of God**.[22]

In the Apocryphal Gospel of St John it is stated: 'If thou hadst known how to suffer thou wouldst have been able not to suffer.' By 'letting go' we are able to experience the sacred dimension of our being that is God's domain. This is the true meaning of Faith. It is also what Jesus was asking of his followers when he said:

> And why take ye thought for raiment? Consider the lilies of the field, how they grow, they toil not, neither do they spin. And yet I say unto you, that even Solomon in all his glory was not arrayed like one of these.[23]

The difficulty once again is that we cannot arrive at such states of trust by simply wanting to. By intention alone and without 'awareness', it becomes blind faith based on superstition. This is the case with most conventional religious practice. Trust of a spiritual nature is not a condition we can impose on ourselves. It is the experience of the unity and 'rightness' of everything that awareness alone can give us. Only then can we find the inner security we search for fruitlessly in the material world. With it comes the unshakeable conviction that we are part of a universal force in which we can place our trust. Call it God, Yahweh, the Buddha-head, Atman, it's of no consequence. By this experience of self-transcendence, allegiance to the ego has been replaced by a far more powerful and benign source of being. Without believing in a 'God' necessarily, life becomes spiritual.

Change emerging from the inside pre-empts the need to impose it from the outside. This being so, no longer would there be the need for a massive military establishment in the world or the force of arms to bring about change. The world is in a permanently precarious state because such methods are no longer viable. The Russian retreat from Afghanistan as well as America's experience in Vietnam, Iraq and now in Afghanistan bear this out beyond any doubt. The cruel dictatorships of North Korea, Burma and Zimbabwe will all terminate sooner or later. No suppression of the human spirit can endure forever. Even China will move towards democracy with time. Spirituality and politics have never been considered a likely combination and yet there are some important examples in history where such politics has been successful. Gandhi, for example, brought about independence for India in this manner. The most powerful empire on earth at the time was obliged to recognise that what he stood for was the force of Truth and that such a force could never be vanquished by arms. It is legitimate to doubt that the Chinese would do the same today in Tibet. But who knows what can happen in the future? Take the case of South Africa's transition to black rule. Nelson Mandela, emerging from many years of captivity at the hands of the white South African authorities, as leader of the new black nation, saw fit to establish the Truth and Reconciliation Commission as a means of overcoming apartheid's legacy of hatred. Based as it was on the biblical values of forgiveness and redemption, Mandela also proved that spiritual principles instituted in the right manner, can have extraordinary, un-hoped for results in the world. Vaclav Havel's courageous resistance to the communist regime in the former Czechoslovakia and the subsequent inspiring leadership of this former writer, thinker and poet is another example. Likewise, Mikhail Gorbachev's decision to lower the Iron Curtain and disband the Soviet Union would not have been taken by a man less wise than he.

In the present state of consciousness of the world, it is hard to imagine this taking place on a global scale. As individuals, in the conduct of our daily lives, however, it is always possible for any one of us to 'be the change we want to see in the world', as Gandhi said. Some already have. In fact, change of this nature can *only* emerge from the base of the social pyramid, one individual at a time. Most people believe that without an ego-centric approach to life we would become vulnerable to the selfish and predatory habits of others. This fear is completely unfounded. An egoist has no leverage whatsoever over a person liberated from his ego. The latter has nothing to prove, no image to uphold, no false ideas about himself to defend, in a word, no pride. Spirituality is the greatest source of strength on earth. Although such people are still rare in the world, the numbers are growing. There are not enough yet to have a visible impact on life as we know it but this will come. It is our collective destiny. We have nothing to lose but our illusions and the fear and insecurities they engender. E. F. Schumacher, at the time of one of the worst post-war recessions, summed this all up over thirty years ago by writing:

Faith in modern man's omnipotence is wearing thin. Even if all the 'new' problems were solved by technological fixes, the state of futility, disorder, and corruption would remain. It existed before the present crises became acute, and it will not go away by itself. More and more people are beginning to realise that the 'modern experiment' has failed…Man closed the gates of Heaven (the spiritual world) against himself and tried with immense energy and ingenuity, to confine himself to the Earth. He is now discovering that the Earth is but a transitory state, so that a **refusal to reach for Heaven means an involuntary descent into Hell.**[24]

XVIII

A relatively common condition in life is that of the egoic mind acting in the interest of others and trying to be 'good'. Conditioned by conventional standards of 'morality', many people devote themselves to good causes and, in general, behave 'decently'. It's an undeniable fact that hundreds of millions of people on earth would rather be good than bad. How is it then that we don't live in an earthly paradise? The answer is that, praise-worthy as this is at one level, it rarely happens as a result of a change of consciousness. Does this matter since the act is well intentioned and the result is positive anyway? Yes. It does. It is our orientation away from the personal identification with our actions that is absolutely crucial. Whilst we remain attached to their perceived desirability, nothing changes. The reason is simple. In normal linear thinking there is a cause and effect relationship between intentions and achieving results. Although this works well in the material world, in the spiritual world it's the opposite. By having intentions, making resolutions, exercising one's will, we tend to strengthen the role of the ego no matter how well meaning our actions. Spirituality comes with the understanding that we are not the prime movers of things in the Universe. By relinquishing the 'sovereignty' of our will we become free, detached and taken up by an energy that leaves us feeling, incomprehensibly, 'full'. This is the mystical meaning of the words 'Thy Will be done' from the Lord's Prayer. On the surface, nothing changes. We continue to make rational decisions and take expedient actions as before, but we do so in a state of detachment, of fearlessness. You can still be a good father and mother, a corporate leader or even a politician but everything you then do in the world is of secondary importance. Only 'being' matters. 'Being' is our security. As Anthony de Mello, the Jesuit spiritual teacher, wrote in his last meditations:

> You will be a creator, when there is abandonment in you — no greed, no ambition, no anxiety, no sense of striving, gaining, arriving, and attaining. All there is, is a keen, penetrating, vigilant awareness that causes the dissolution of one's foolishness and selfishness, all of one's attachments and fears. The changes that follow are not the result of your blueprints and efforts but the product of nature (God) that spurns your plans and will leave no room for a sense of merit or achievement or even any consciousness on the part of your left hand of what reality is doing by means of your right.[25]

G. I. Gurdjieff, made an important distinction between knowledge and being that is critical to this question. Knowledge, he said, is the product of thought and intellect whereas being is a combination of feelings and instincts associated with our spiritual nature as well. Only the synthesis of the two produces a certain quality of understanding that goes beyond the theoretical constructs of the mind. This more holistic intelligence is capable of grasping *not only the form but also the meaning of things*. In our increasingly scientific and technological world, the split between knowledge and being has become ever wider. The extreme limitation of the materialist way of thinking is to believe that all our problems, even those of a psychological nature, can have material solutions — more social programmes, more teachers, better housing, lower interest rates and so on. This lopsided intelligence, reflecting a one-dimensional view of life, is brought to bear on every issue. When the younger generations demonstrate against globalization today, they do so for the same reason those similar generations dropped out in the 1960's. They are reacting to a suffocating materialism that propagates a soulless form of progress throughout the world. As things are, this cannot be avoided. Without higher levels of consciousness, these karmic patterns will continue to be repeated. A reading of the great books, and in particular the plays of William Shakespeare, reveals to us that questions of honour, loyalty, sacrifice, redemption, retribution, humility, wisdom and love were the major recurring themes in literature as in life. It suggests that there was a time when the search for moral purpose and meaning was a vital human need.

In modern society, all this now seems to have vanished giving way to the shameless, self-centred, free-for-all we witness today. The unrepentant claim on totally unjustified levels of compensation in the corporate world clearly reveals this pathological form of selfishness at work. It has recently come to light, for example, that a Forbes 500 CEO on average earns in two hours what the lowest paid employees of the same company makes in a year. Can the labour of any man or women on earth be worth two thousand times that of a fellow worker? Although an aberration of this order is morally repugnant and indefensible, the social system most of us live by, vote for, pay our taxes to sustain and send our young soldiers out to die for, has consistently failed to sanction it. In a time of severe economic difficulty for many, it is like grabbing seats on the lifeboats of the Titanic as the women and children drown. As a result, the gap between the rich and poor, already at unacceptable levels in the U.S and UK continues to widen. In America, fifty million people have been obliged to live without health insurance. In the richest nation on earth, unable to afford treatment, people die prematurely or are condemned to infirmity every day. Unless the planned changes founder, we shall see to what degree Barack Obama's proposed Healthcare Plan will change this.

XIX

It is stated in the scriptures that 'God will not be mocked' (Galatians: 6 7-9). The meaning of these words is very straightforward. We can't contravene the laws of the universe, our essential nature, without suffering the consequences. The Buddhist concept of Karma operates in much the same way. Bearing in mind that in the short history of humanity the Perennial Philosophy has been largely disregarded, one can only assume that the problems the world has been experiencing of late are a mere precursor of what is to come. The laws of cause and effect operate in a moral universe every bit as much as they do in an empirical one. There is often a lengthy time lag between an original cause and its subsequent effect that can give the impression that there will be no day of reckoning. This is misleading. The immense material and technological power that has developed over the last hundred and fifty years is now accelerating and amplifying the repercussions of events set in motion decades ago. In less than fifty years, for example, we have done more lasting damage to the planet than in the entire history of mankind. If substantial changes don't take place in the way we live and utilize the diminishing resources at our disposal, by this measure alone the time remaining to us will be short.

A thousand years ago this wasn't the case. People could plunder and kill each other with abandon without serious consequences to the planet. Blood thirsty and murderous as human history certainly was, the ecological balance of nature was not being threatened. This is no longer true today. The first decades of the 21st century should be viewed as a crossroads for humanity. We must alter our ways or risk the eventuality that cataclysmic change will be forced upon us in a far shorter period of time than we dare to believe. Some of the younger generation seems to have taken this to heart. Their ambitions have been modified by what they see going on in the world. The post-war baby boom generation, having been spared the great wars of the 20th century, embraced a period of unprecedented growth in prosperity with an enthusiasm that blinded them to its consequences. Subsequent generations are now obliged to take stock of the situation with a greater sense of responsibility. There is now a growing realisation among some young people that reaping the benefits of a highly localized and unequally distributed prosperity is no longer a worthy ambition. On the contrary, more and more now feel that they must be of service to society. Organisations such as Amnesty International and Doctors Without Borders make an extraordinary contribution to human well being. When I think of their selfless work across the world I salute their courage and dedication and momentarily question all I have just written. It's only by being obliged to acknowledge that such people are, regrettably, a tiny minority that doesn't represent the spirit of our times that I feel justified in writing this book. They do, however, incarnate hope for the future.

In the course of history, mankind has managed to overcome extraordinary material and moral challenges. Tyranny has been banished from many parts of the world, many mortal diseases that decimated populations no longer exist, life spans have more than doubled, a lasting peace has taken root in the world's traditional theatre of conflict (Europe), international organisations have been established to provide economic assistance to poor countries and many people in the world can now rely on a system of justice and the rule of law. These worthy accomplishments have been arrived at by means of human intelligence and our capacity for reason. Effective an instrument as it may be, this form of intelligence has always been a double-edged sword. The same intelligence that split the atom and transplants hearts also developed nuclear weapons and bacterial warfare. The missing ingredient capable of guiding our choices is wisdom.

Unfortunately, this pre-eminent and most rare of human virtues remains elusive. We can will ourselves to become kind, fair, patient, loyal, steadfast, trustworthy and loving but we can't become wise for the wanting. Without transcending the ego there can be no wisdom. Nevertheless, humanity possesses immense resources of good will. At present, estrangement from our spiritual nature prevents us from using this precious resource to its best effect. If we can harness it by overcoming our egoism, as a growing number of people have done, it's not too late to change course. 'Hope', as Vaclav Havel pointed out, 'is not the conviction that something will turn out well but the certainty that it makes sense.' For this reason, hope can never be abandoned. Nevertheless, a profound change of heart is required on a scale as yet unseen in the world. It is possible that the challenging times ahead will oblige us to alter our whole perspective on what to expect from life. Adversity will chip away at comfortable lives and attitudes until we finally 'let go' of our egoism and discover what constitutes our essential humanity. This is the only development possible for mankind and our chance of survival in the long run, global warming or not. At this point in time, of course, I can quite understand that few would agree with this hypothesis.

In this brief reflection I have tried to indicate in as many ways as I know how, that the ego, by obscuring the need to change, is not only an obstacle to our survival in the future but to our happiness in the present. In this hapless quest to secure happiness, we have complicated our lives beyond comprehension, whereas only in inner and outer simplicity can it be found. The rewards, therefore, are immense and proportionate to the challenge. By demanding less, we should be ready to give more. Instead of using nature as a dispensable commodity, we can respect our natural environment, conserve its beauty and sense our affiliation to it. Free of egoism we can learn to love with our souls and live without pride. The wasteful affluence of some would give way to an equitable, peaceful and dignified life for all. Simplicity in our personal lives would allow the de-humanising complexity of society to reverse itself naturally, restoring to its members physical health and psychological 'wholeness'. Lastly, by healing this bountiful planet of ours, we would start constituting the only inheritance that can have any significance for future generations. In doing so, we would also come to the understanding that far from having the unquestioned right to life on this earth, we must first deserve it.

The man of Tao
Remains unknown
Perfect virtue
Produces nothing
'No-Self'
Is 'True-Self'
And the greatest man
Is Nobody.

Chuang Tzu (xviii. 3)

Afterword

By way of a sincere response to those who believe that I have been overly pessimistic in my assessment of the state of the world and the likely prospects for humanity, I would say that there is nothing I would like more than to be proved wrong. Believing in a spiritual reality, as I do, means that I also believe in the potential of man to surpass himself and become God-like, as all the scriptures claim. This is his true destiny.

The greatest difficulty for me in understanding the mystery of life is why there are so many obstacles preventing us from the realisation of this essential truth. Flowers, plants and animals, for example, develop naturally and fulfil their destinies effortlessly. Man is the exception in the universe. The difference, many say, lies in the fact that we have freewill. This, I find to be an unsatisfactory explanation. It doesn't, for example, explain why, in the case of humanity it is the *wrong* habits of living that are acquired naturally and effortlessly whereas the right ones call for a lifetime of unrelenting effort. Like Alaskan salmon it seems that we are obliged to swim against the current to reach our spawning grounds. Some will argue that for a 'higher' destiny to exist there must also be a 'lower' one. Freewill exists so as to give us the possibility of going one way or the other. 'God provides the wind but Man must raise the sails,' said St Augustine. It is when the lower destiny is mistaken for the higher one, which is the case today that the difficulties mount. You are then not just swimming uphill in a fast flowing stream but you are having to leap up rapids and waterfalls.

With four children starting out in the world, I hope with every fibre of my being that we find a way to pull the rabbit out of the hat in time to prevent the worst. Whether this occurs through a sudden and miraculous transformation of human nature or some other form of divine intervention, is of no consequence. What is important is to prove that the German philosopher Schopenhauer was wrong when he announced once that 'life is something that should not have been'.

Notes

(Parts of quotations shown in bold type are those of the author, and do not appear in the original quotations.)

CHAPTER II
1 Jung, Carl, *Without faith, No Meaning,*
   International Herald Tribune, 1986

CHAPTER III
2 Tolle, Eckhart, *A New Earth: Awakening to Your Life's Purpose,*
   Chapter 4, (Plume Edition, 2006)

CHAPTER IV
3 Tobin, James, *International Herald Tribune* article,
   November 2009
4 Sayers, Dorothy L., *Introductory Papers on Dante,*
   Page 114, (London, 1954)

CHAPTER V
5 Bloom, Allan, *The Closing of the American Mind,*
   (Simon & Schuster, 1987)
6 Bellow, Saul, *International Herald Tribune* article, 1985

CHAPTER VIII
7 Schumacher, Ernst F., *Small is Beautiful*, Chapter 4,
   (Harper & Row Edition, 1975)

CHAPTER IX
8 Isaacson, Walter, *Einstein & Faith, Time* magazine Article,
   April 5, 2007
9 Schumacher, Ernst F., *A Guide for the Perplexed*, Chapter 9,
   (Harper Perennial, 1977)
10 Merton, Thomas, *The Way of Chuang Tzu*, (Allen & Unwin
   Edition, 1970)

CHAPTER X

11 Tolle, Eckhart, *A New Earth: Awakening to Your Life's Purpose,*
Chapter 7, (Plume Edition, 2006)

12 Picasso, Pablo, *Letter to Giovanni Papini,* C.I.C.E.S.
Rue de la Sante, Paris, 153

13 Joachim Gasquet, *Cezanne-A Memoir with Conversations*, p 150.
Thames and Hudson. London.1991..

14 Joachim Gasquet, *Cezanne-A Memoir with Conversations*, p 150.
Thames and Hudson. London.1991.

CHAPTER XI

15 Suzuki, D. T., *Introduction to Zen by Eugene Herrigel,*
(McGraw Hill Edition, 1964)

16 Suzuki, Shunryu, *Zen Mind, Beginner's Mind*, p21
(Weatherhill Edition, 1973)

17 Herrigel, Eugene, *The Method of Zen*, p 100, (McGraw Hill
Edition, 1964)

18 Nicoll, Maurice, *Psychological Commentaries Vol. 3*, p 865,
(Stuart Edition, 1957)

CHAPTER XII

19 Berry, Wendell, *The Unsettling of America,* p 20, (Sierra Club
Books Edition, 1977)

CHAPTER XIII

20 Gurdjieff, G. I., *Meetings with Remarkable Men: Introduction,*
(Dutton Edition, 1974)

CHAPTER XV

21 Berry, Wendell, *The Unsettling of America: Introduction*, p 6,
(Sierra Club Books, 1977)

CHAPTER XVII

22 Bennett. J. G., *Intimations*, pp 43-44 (Beshara Publications, 1975)

23 Matthew 6: 28-29, *The Holy Bible: New Testament,*
(New Revised Standard Edition)

24 Schumacher, Ernst F., *A Guide for the Perplexed: Epilogue,*
(Harper Perennial, 1977)

CHAPTER XVIII

25 De Mello, Anthony, *The Way To Love: The Last Meditations,*
(Doubleday Edition, 1995)

Bibliography

Allen Bloom *The Closing of the American Mind*

Wendell Berry *The Unsettling of America*

E. F. Schumacher *Small is Beautiful*

E. F. Schumacher *A Guide for the Perplexed*

Eugen Herrigel *Zen in the Art of Archery*

Eugen Herrigel *The Method of Zen*

P. D. Ouspensky *In Search of the Miraculous*

P. D Ouspensky *The Psychology of Man's Possible Evolution*

Aldous Huxley *The Perennial Philosophy*

Fyodor Dostoevsky *The Idiot*

Maurice Nicoll *Psychological Commentaries*

G. I. Gurdjieff *Meetings with Remarkable Men*

Thomas Merton *The Seven Story Mountain*

Thomas Merton *The Way of Chuang Tzu*

Shunryu Suzuki *Zen Mind Beginner's Mind*

Anthony De Mello *Awareness*

John Robbins *Diet for a New America*

T.S. Eliot *Burnt Norton*

James George *Asking For The Earth*

W. B. Yeats *The Second Coming*

Erich Fromm *The Art of Loving*